IMAGES
of America

LOS ANGELES'S
ORIGINAL FARMERS MARKET

ON THE COVER: The original Farmers Market began when two entrepreneurs had an idea, which they presented to Earl Bell Gilmore in 1934. Their idea led to the creation of one of Los Angeles's most cherished destinations. In the 1940s, the A. F. Gilmore Company paid tribute to the idea by placing the words on one of its iconic clock towers. (Courtesy A. F. Gilmore Company.)

IMAGES
of America

LOS ANGELES'S
ORIGINAL FARMERS MARKET

David Hamlin and Brett Arena

ARCADIA
PUBLISHING

Published by Arcadia Publishing
Charleston SC, Chicago IL, Portsmouth NH, San Francisco CA

Printed in the United States of America

Library of Congress Control Number: 2009921931

For all general information contact Arcadia Publishing at:
Telephone 843-853-2070
Fax 843-853-0044
E-mail sales@arcadiapublishing.com
For customer service and orders:
Toll-Free 1-888-313-2665

Visit us on the Internet at www.arcadiapublishing.com

There are two kinds of people,
those who cherish Farmers Market
and those who have not yet experienced it.
This book is dedicated to the former.
The latter, we hope, will be inspired to visit soon.

CONTENTS

ACKNOWLEDGMENTS

From the day they arrived at the 256-acre ranch at Third Street and Fairfax Avenue in Los Angeles, the A. F. Gilmore family have been thoughtful, innovative, and responsible stewards. From Arthur Fremont Gilmore forward through four generations, the property has been carefully preserved, protected, and enhanced. Their care and dedication created Farmers Market. Their contribution to the city of Los Angeles and its people and to millions around the world is gratefully acknowledged.

So, too, is their commitment to history. The Gilmore family has provided all the images in this book. They have scrupulously maintained a treasure trove of family documents, photographs, maps, correspondence, and memorabilia that tell the story of the land and all it has generated. The current stewards of Farmers Market—Hank Hilty and the A. F. Gilmore Company Board of Directors, Mark Panatier, Ilysha Buss, and a remarkably dedicated and skillful staff—all informed this book. Carol Newsom and the staff at Newsom Design provided valuable support as well.

Roger Dahlhjelm, a remarkable fellow, and Fred Beck, a promoter and publicist who had more flair than most, are both, in spirit and inspiration, in every Market story.

Brett Arena is the A. F. Gilmore Company archivist. His joy in his work and his deep respect and admiration for the history he charts are inspiring.

The merchants of Farmers Market are its heart and soul.

The author also salutes Sydney Weisman, who takes me to the most wonderful places and who introduced me to Farmers Market.

Unless otherwise credited, all of the images contained in this book are drawn from and courtesy of the A. F. Gilmore Company.

—David Hamlin

INTRODUCTION

At every turn, that which Los Angeles needed, Farmers Market provided.

In 1934, Los Angeles was in the grip of the Great Depression. When 18 entrepreneurs, guided by two inspired innovators and a successful businessman, launched Farmers Market, it was instantly a symbol of hope, a demonstration that things could and would get better. Their success sparked an economic engine, a source of employment, and a smart, sensible option for consumers. As the economy began to right itself, Farmers Market led the way.

Los Angeles grew up and out for two reasons—there was land on which to grow and there was ample fuel to allow those who lived across the expanses to move about. That fuel was Gilmore Oil, which powered West Coast vehicles and helped pave its roads from the beginning of the 20th century well into the middle of it. The petroleum products that enabled the city to grow flowed from the land where Farmers Market rose.

Los Angeles became the magnet for movies and stars—Farmers Market became their place. Before the Market rose on the land that had been the Gilmore dairy farm before oil was discovered, portions of *The Four Horsemen of the Apocalypse* had been filmed there, the earliest sign that Hollywood and the Farmers Market would be best friends. Over the years, the Market would become a place where stars could dine and shop and a natural habitat for writers to create, directors to plan, and workaday crew members—grips, cameramen, production assistants, best boys, makeup artists—to mingle and meet.

Through the 20th century, Los Angeles became the nation's multicultural destination. It drew new residents from every section of the United States and millions of immigrants from the world around. Farmers Market reflected and celebrated that diversity. Its restaurants, from the first, implacably Irish, to those that followed, all mirrored the city they serve. Asian and Italian dishes, East Coast deli and Southern fare, Mexican, mid-Eastern and Brazilian meals all cross Market counters; all who seek their own special cuisine come to Farmers Market to find it.

Roasted mixed nuts were invented at the Market, and the first pizzeria in Southern California opened here. Trendy, stylish California chefs prepare meals next door to burger and hot dog shops. The world came to Los Angeles to live; its people came to the Market to eat.

Los Angeles was not the sporting mecca it would later become when the Market opened, but it was no less a sports town. Mere months before it opened, and for decades after, Farmers Market was next door to the center of L.A.'s sporting life. Here was a home to professional baseball and football, an auto racing empire, even an occasional boxing bout or cricket match, all nourishing the city's love of sports.

In the earliest days of television, which eventually grew to become a cultural and economic force so potent that it all but defined Los Angeles, it was an East Coast medium. The center of the industry moved abruptly and emphatically west to Los Angeles when CBS created Television City on Farmers Market property. In the explosion of television programming that followed the advent of cable, Farmers Market became a studio itself, the location of countless productions featuring everything from chefs to game shows to interviews to would-be singing and dancing stars.

For three-quarters of a century, Los Angeles has depended on Farmers Market. Families have returned again and again to the Market for celebrations, politicians seeking citywide office dare not neglect it, renowned chefs shop nowhere else, PTA moms meet at the Market, business associates lunch here, musicians and their fans commune at the Market, and groups of friends gather at the Market so regularly that they have their "own" tables.

The inextricable bond that weds Los Angeles to its favorite place arises from the one magnificent characteristic that has defined Farmers Market from its very first days—Farmers Market changes constantly even as it remains essentially the same. In a city vigorously dedicated to bringing down a building in order to erect a new one, Farmers Market has been the one true constant. It is the city's most stable resident, its most reliable venue, and its oldest friend. Farmers Market is as strong and as vibrant and as permanent as the land on which it sits.

The history of Farmers Market is no more or less a history of modern Los Angeles. It is rich, compelling, bright, and sunny. It is the very best of Los Angeles.

One

AN IDEA

In 1934, in the heart of the Great Depression, two entrepreneurs, Roger Dahlhjelm and Fred Beck, approached Earl Bell (E. B.) Gilmore with an idea. Dahlhjelm (Doll-yum), who worked in the Happy Oven Bakery in Hollywood, and Beck, an advertising copywriter, wanted to create a village square that would provide artisans with an open-air market in which they could create and sell their wares. They also proposed inviting local farmers to set up stalls in the center of the square once or twice a week; the farmers would sell farm-fresh produce to local housewives.

E. B. Gilmore was the chief executive of his family's business, the A. F. Gilmore Company. The family owned a substantial piece of property at the corner of Third Street and Fairfax Avenue in Los Angeles. The property had been a dairy farm until E. B. Gilmore's father, Arthur Fremont Gilmore, began drilling for water and discovered oil. An enormous oil field replaced the dairy herd, producing crude oil for the Gilmore Oil Company until local regulations banned oil rigs in residential communities. By 1934, although Gilmore Oil was still the mainstay of the family business, the land was little more than a very large vacant lot.

E. B. Gilmore was not interested in the "Village Square" proposal that Dahlhjelm and Beck presented, but he was intrigued by the notion of a market for farmers. He gave them permission to invite local farmers to park their trucks on the empty land and Dahlhjelm and Beck set about recruiting farmers.

In July 1934, a dozen farmers and a handful of other merchants parked their trucks at the corner of Third Street and Fairfax Avenue and launched what its two creators called the Farmers Public Market.

The idea was an enormous success. In a matter of weeks, makeshift stalls replaced the trucks, and in mere months, Los Angeles was enjoying shopping and dining at Farmers Market. The "idea" quickly became L.A.'s favorite place. It remains so today, 75 years later.

Arthur Fremont Gilmore and Julius Carter purchased the large rancho near the La Brea Tar Pits in 1880. It was a working farm, seen here under cultivation. Eventually the two men decided to dissolve their partnership. To do so, they drew straws and A. F. Gilmore became the sole proprietor of what would become known as "Gilmore Island" in Los Angeles.

Gilmore Island was originally part of an enormous land grant owned by Antonio Jose Rocha, a Portuguese immigrant. When he died, the estate was in disarray and one of his tenants, James Thompson, came into possession of a large portion of the land. When Thompson's enterprise failed, A. F. Gilmore and Julius Carter bought it in 1880.

Arthur Fremont (A. F.) Gilmore lived in the original adobe farmhouse, built in 1852. He and Julius Carter had a thriving dairy farm in Compton, California. They established another on the land they secured from James Thompson and it, too, grew to be most successful. The adobe home remains today, an oasis in the center of metropolitan Los Angeles. Earl Bell Gilmore lived there, and it remains headquarters for the A. F. Gilmore Company today.

The Gilmore property was a working farm and the Gilmore adobe was both a family home and a bunkhouse. When A. F. Gilmore decided to expand his dairy herd, the expansion required more water and he set about drilling for it. He found oil.

The discovery of oil on Gilmore Island produced rapid and dramatic changes. The dairy herd quickly disappeared, replaced by a huge oil field and dozens of derricks. The petroleum was used primarily for lubricants and paving material when it was first discovered, but soon after the beginning of the 20th century, it would become the fuel that drove the explosive growth of the West, powering cars and trucks up and down the West Coast.

While the A. F. Gilmore Company was growing and thriving, Roger Dahlhjelm had left his home in Minnesota in search of his own success. He sold land in the Midwest, operated a Stanley Steamer franchise in Seattle, and then came to Los Angeles as a land developer. His efforts in L.A. did not fare at all well, and by 1934, he was earning exactly $4 a week and all the baked goods he could consume as a bookkeeper for the Happy Oven in Hollywood.

Arthur Fremont Gilmore and his son Earl Bell stand in front of the large oil field that dominated the family's former dairy farm at the turn of the 20th century. E. B. became chief executive of the family business and drove the company to new heights, marketing and promoting Gilmore Oil with a mixture of savvy and flair that placed the company's products squarely in the minds and the vocabulary of the people in the western United States.

Pictured here from left to right are Fred Beck, Roger Dahlhjelm, and E. B. Gilmore. When the two entrepreneurs proposed their "idea" to Gilmore, he rejected most of the concept but agreed that creating a market for farmers at Third Street and Fairfax Avenue in Los Angeles was worth trying. Dahlhjelm and Beck recruited the farmers and Beck, in particular, found ingenious ways to promote the idea on a shoestring budget.

Farmers Market opened in July 1934. The initial group of farmers paid 50¢ to park their trucks on the vacant Gilmore land. Los Angeles area shoppers were so taken with fresh fruits and vegetables in a casual, sunny venue like the open-air market that it was an instant success. By August, Roger Dahlhjelm and Fred Beck were already turning the place into something permanent. They fashioned an unusual scheme. E. B. Gilmore had built a dog-racing track before the Market opened, but the licenses for it were never secured. So Roger Dahlhjelm contacted a handyman and turned him loose on the track's facade. They scavenged lumber and dragged it over to the Market to build stalls for the farmers. There is no evidence that Dahlhjelm had permission to do this, but the result was stability. The Farmers Market was permanent.

From the very first day of Farmers Market, Roger Dahlhjelm imposed strict standards on the farmers. Fred Beck's radio advertisements, written to recruit farmers to the new market, threatened to throw anyone out who did not deliver the freshest possible produce. Dahlhjelm actually did just that in the first days of the Market, ejecting a farmer who tried to sell tomatoes he had purchased at a local grocery store when his own homegrown supply ran out.

Although the farmers and their produce were at the heart of the original Farmers Market, other merchants soon arrived to take advantage of the steady flow of consumers who were quickly embracing the place. Restaurants arrived, including a malt shop that offered the popular soda fountain treat for a dime.

15

Fred Beck's first radio advertisements soliciting farmers to the Market stressed the fact that only farm-fresh, same-day produce would be accepted. The advertisements not only drew farmers, they convinced housewives that shopping at the Market would make their meals terrific. Beck took advantage of the idea by creating an impromptu parade of farmers with wheelbarrows—note that one of the signs says its driver was ejected from the Market for failing to meet the rigorous standards. (Photograph by Don Milton.)

When Farmers Market first opened, it had no restrooms. Instead, a shuttle carried customers from the Market to nearby Gilmore Stadium (see chapter 4) where they could avail themselves of the facilities. The arrangement, however cumbersome, satisfied sanitation rules. Soon enough, at the urging of Blanche Magee, who opened the first restaurant at Farmers Market, restrooms were installed on site.

By fall of 1934, Farmers Market was successful enough and had enough promotional funds available to start capitalizing on its popularity. Fred Beck and Roger Dahlhjelm organized a Fall Festival to celebrate the harvest. They prevailed on the Market's merchants to create makeshift "floats" using the shuttle carts that carried produce to and from the stalls and created an eccentric parade.

Fall Festival featured a family-friendly event—the cow-milking contest. Fall Festival at Farmers Market, originally a four-day affair, eventually dwindled down to two days but, with the sole exception of a brief hiatus during World War II, the festival has been part of the Market's annual schedule of events from the very first year.

Pumpkins for sale! Fall Festival at Farmers Market almost always features a pumpkin patch in honor of its proximity to Halloween. Similarly, the parade gave rise to a tradition that remains to this day—Market merchants dressing in costumes that highlight either the rustic origins of the Market or celebrate Halloween.

Although this photograph was taken about a decade after the opening of Farmers Market, it honors that opening. All those gathered for this photograph are original Farmers Market merchants, farmers, chefs, and vendors who helped to create the institution and turn it into one of the most popular destinations on the West Coast.

Fred Beck was the genius behind a vast array of promotions that made Farmers Market so popular. He constantly created stunts and events to generate publicity for the Market. In this somewhat unusual, but certainly typical, Beck adventure, he is either awarding the winner in a contest he dreamt up or auctioning the cuddly feline to a winning bidder.

This aerial portrait of Farmers Market is from its earliest days. Gilmore Stadium (chapter 4) is in the background. The Market had quickly become a solid, permanent facility, with meandering aisles and permanent stalls fed by water and power (neither of which were available when the Market first opened).

One of the original icons that identified Farmers Market for those motoring past or pulling onto its acres of parking was a windmill, which became part of the Market's culture when the name was painted on it. The windmill eventually gave way to the Farmers Market clock towers as the primary icons for the property.

Farmers Market was from the beginning an utterly unique blend of rustic and urban. While the farmers were part of a still agrarian Los Angeles, the Market itself was in the center of what was becoming a metropolitan area. This shot captures that extraordinary marriage—the Market, amidst a growing city, framed by the pristine Hollywood Hills and the Santa Monica mountain range. (Photograph by Dick Whittington.)

The Market moved quickly beyond its produce-on-trucks stage and soon other merchants sought to join the enterprise. Campbell Stewart approached Roger Dahlhjelm about opening a full grocery store. Dahlhjelm, still operating the Market on an informal agreement with E. B. Gilmore, had no reserves to fund construction. So he persuaded Stewart to put up a deposit of one year's rent in advance and used those funds as collateral for a construction loan. Stewart could secure a refund during his first year, but he succeeded and remained at the Market for quite some time. This unusual financing scheme was employed for several other stores in the Market's early history. The rest of the stalls and shops operated on 30-day tenancies and, to this day, many Market stalls remain on that month-to-month arrangement—some have done so for decades. (Photograph by Dick Whittington.)

Within a few years, Farmers Market had developed into a popular shopping venue and a destination for diners and shoppers from Los Angeles and beyond. The parking lots surrounding the Market had grown more organized and additional buildings had been constructed to augment the stalls and shops inside the Farmers Market itself. In a remarkably short period of time, especially given the harsh economic climate in which it began, Farmers Market was a roaring success. (Photograph by Dick Whittington.)

Two

Meet Me at
Third and Fairfax

Farmers Market enjoyed remarkable success from its earliest days. Surprisingly, given the dire economic straits the nation was in when the Market first opened, it did steady and solid business right from the start. As a result, the original farmers were soon keeping company with merchants of all sorts selling customers everything from flowers and decorated gourds to candy and magazines. A grocery store joined the Market and so did a wide and increasingly varied array of restaurants. Within a few years, the Farmers Market offered Irish fare, a fish and chips stand, delis, roasted chicken, and more.

The Farmers Market also grew in a hurry and, like a teen, awkwardly and in spurts. The original materials that became the Market's first stalls were actually scavenged—Roger Dahlhjelm hired the handyman from the Happy Oven and sent him off to dismantle and salvage a dog-racing track that E. B. Gilmore had built on the property. Dahlhjelm, whether with permission or not, simply swiped lumber and awnings to create his Farmers Market.

As the growth spurt proceeded, Farmers Market aisles meandered among vegetables and candy stores, one right next to the other; and the aisles also wandered past dining tables and kitchens, only to stop abruptly and take a hard turn one way or the other. Power lines snaked here and there—even today, some wiring in the Market is akin to an electrician's worst dreams—and the place quickly became a full-grown character in its own right.

It also became a Hollywood destination. Early on, a few stars, including Gail Patrick and Greta Garbo, fell for the place and local columnists (Hedda Hopper and Louella Parsons, for example) noted their affection in print. Soon Hollywood press agents were squiring would-be starlets to the Market for publicity shots; those hopefuls would usually pass other actors, directors, writers, and everyday Hollywood laborers who used the Farmers Market to take meetings, shop, or simply relax and eat.

That Hollywood connection merged with the charming ambiance and the endless variety of cuisines to turn Farmers Market into a destination for locals and tourists alike. Within 10 years, Roger Dahlhjelm and Fred Beck had achieved their original revenue projections ($6 million annually) and Farmers Market was the number-one tourist destination in Los Angeles.

This is a classic Farmers Market photograph, one that has been used to promote the Market for years. It features a couple of somewhat bedazzled customers standing amidst the hustle of business, the quirky collection of stalls and shops, and the steady flow of visitors and shoppers who came to the Market every day (save Sunday—the Market was not open on Sundays until 1983).

Thompson's Juice Stand was one of the many produce stalls that helped drive the Market's initial success. Loaded with fresh products and staffed by friendly folks who, more often than not, had grown or created the products available at their counters, Thompson's was a typical Farmers Market enterprise.

Farmers Market celebrated its first anniversary in 1935. By then, it was fully realized—restaurants offered fresh meals and diners could sit beneath umbrellas and enjoy the food and the passing parade. When the Market first opened, there were no tables or chairs—it was Blanche Magee, the merchant who opened the Market's first restaurant, who insisted on seating.

Fall Festival at Farmers Market was part of the place from the very beginning and so was music. In addition to concerts and an occasional itinerate musician (for years, a violin player was as much a part of the Market as its apples and oranges), Fred Beck and Roger Dahlhjelm hired country bands to enhance their harvest celebration.

This classic Farmers Market scene features a well-stocked fruit stand, contented shoppers, and friendly merchants behind the counter. The combination of readily available fresh produce, fruits, meats, and poultry and the opportunity to stop for lunch or a snack in the middle of a grocery-shopping excursion made the Farmers Market all but irresistible to local housewives.

Among the many fruit and vegetable stands, the Farmers Market provided a wide range of other experiences. Manning's Coffee and Tea was a typical shop, and its location was a classic example of the way in which the Market grew. Note that, hard by the coffee shop, corn stalks are displayed at the shop next door.

The A. C. Cordester fruit and vegetable stand was one of the earlier successful Market stalls. Although it was situated among a dozen or more just like it, this shop could easily have been a roadside farmer's stand—rustic and entirely agrarian. Indeed, when Roger Dahlhjelm and Fred Beck first set out to recruit farmers for their "idea," they visited many roadside stands to lure farmers to a more commodious venue.

Gill's Old Fashioned Ice Cream stand was one of the very first non-farmer shops to open at Farmers Market. Like Magee's Kitchen, it is still doing business at the Market, testimony to the amazing longevity and success that several dozen merchants have enjoyed over the years. Note the wicker shopping baskets in front of the stand, which were created to enable grocery shoppers to move from one stall to the next while toting their purchases in arcane-wheeled carts that could be pulled along but would stand upright while people were shopping.

This is an early Farmers Market flower shop. One measure of the early success of Farmers Market was its appeal to merchants vending non-food products. That aspect of the Market emerged very early in its history. As soon as entrepreneurs grew convinced that the Market was not a temporary fad, they began contacting Roger Dahlhjelm seeking space. Dahlhjelm applied his rigorous standards to one and all, but he also welcomed a variety of operators, which, prior to Farmers Market, had rarely been gathered together in a single venue.

Carfora's at Farmers Market sold Italian food and grocery products. Friendly service came with each and every stop in the Market. Then, as now, merchants— typically the owners of shops are found behind counters—stand ready to provide cooking tips, seasoning advice, shopping guidance, and preparation instructions.

The variety of shops arriving at the Farmers Market in its early years included this open-air drugstore, packed with products and an extensive supply of magazines. The Market grew in a hodgepodge style, and aisles meandered through the shops and stalls. There was little logic to the system—this drugstore was next to a produce stand, a butcher shop stood beside a shop offering decorated gourds, and a roasted chicken counter was next to a candy store. The entire blend was both confusing and entertaining. The aisles of the Farmers Market seemed (as they still do) to have minds of their own. One aisle might move straight from one stall to the next, only to hit a dead-end at a fruit stand. Another took an unexpected jog to the right and all of the aisles were filled not just with shoppers but also with tables and chairs for dining. The Farmers Market has an identity and a sense of character all its own—it was and is truly unique.

In its first years, the Farmers Market closed at 6:00 p.m. In 1936, the Hollywood Women's Press Club sought permission to stage an after-hours fund-raiser for the Red Cross. The concept was simple: the club asked celebrities to work at Market shops with the proceeds going to the charity. Roger Dahlhjelm thought they should charge admission to increase the charitable income and to hold down the crowds; his counsel went unheeded. The event featured more than 80 stars, from Cary Grant to the young and rising Broderick Crawford, pictured here. It also caused a traffic jam that extended for several miles in all directions. Fred Beck described the event as "pandemonium among the parsnips." Cary Grant lost articles of clothing before he reached the stall where he was to work, and Greer Garson needed a police escort to reach her shop.

No star working for the Red Cross at Farmers Market was more popular than Shirley Temple, assigned counter duty at Brock's Candy. The crowd could not resist buying a bon-bon from her and the result was a frenzied crush. The display windows at the shop began to bulge as the eager crowd pressed in and the situation turned from entertaining to perilous. The fire department sought to rescue her, but the large crowd hindered their access to her. The firemen climbed to the roof of the shop and cut a hole through it. In this extraordinary photograph, Shirley Temple remains calm and astonishingly serene before her eager fans; within moments after the photograph was taken, she was hoisted out of the shop just before the display case collapsed, sending glass and candy in all directions.

Within years after they opened the first restaurant at the Farmers Market, the Magee family set up a second shop, Magee's Nuts. There, Blanche Magee applied her ingenuity anew. When supplies of specific nuts were insufficient to sell them alone, Blanche mixed several varieties together and then roasted the mixture. She thus created a new innovation—roasted mixed nuts.

Colonial Kitchens' Exchange offered customers freshly baked goods daily, but it also exemplified the Farmers Market's decidedly quirky nature. The bakeshop stood immediately beside a poultry shop, a juxtaposition that simply did not occur in traditional grocery stores, but which was typical of the Market. The eclectic placement of shops grew entirely by happenstance, but the serendipitous result helped define the Market's character and delighted customers, who found discoveries at every turn.

Shoppers at Farmers Market often found the unexpected. Wenger's Poultry shop sold customers fresh fryers, legs, thighs, and breasts. It also offered an experience unique to Farmers Market, live chickens in the nooks and crannies of the store's display counters. Area housewives could not find such unusual company at their local A&P, but they also had no doubt that the products they purchased at Wenger's were absolutely fresh.

Almost as quickly as it opened, the Farmers Market offered Los Angeles a complete grocery shopping experience at a single stop. In addition to farm-fresh produce, poultry, and meats, seafood was readily available at shops such as Ocean Seafood. The selection and variety at the Farmers Market rivaled traditional grocery stores, but it came with the fun of open-air shopping and a convenient collection of restaurants serving all manner of breakfast and lunch menus.

Roger Dahlhjelm and Fred Beck never stopped promoting the Farmers Market even as it grew more popular and successful. They continued the early promotional event, Fall Festival, and the merchants of the Market carried on its traditions, including donning costumes, which they wore even while behind their counters, for the four-day harvest celebration.

Yank's was a fixture in the Market's early days; Tom Yank was one of the first farmers who sold produce from the beds of pick-up trucks. His stall was immediately next door to A. C. Cordester's, also offering fresh produce. The competition fostered business for all. Many merchants at the Farmers Market carried similar products, yet all did well. Each built a following with steady groups of regulars.

As a means of both drawing customers and making their experience as much fun as possible, music was part of the Farmers Market experience within a few months after it opened. Fall Festivals always featured costumes and floats and a parade, but they also offered bands performing both inside and outside the Market. This band, featuring a shining stand-up bass, entertained passing shoppers at one of the earliest Fall Festivals.

The Farmers Market was, from its earliest days, a family operation in every sense. The Gilmore family was instrumental in creating and supporting the Market and most of the shops and stalls inside were mom-and-pop operations. Dana's, which offered roasted chicken for on-the-spot dining or take-home, was very much part of the family tradition; its owner and operator was Roger Dahlhjelm's sister.

There are two stories about patio dining at Farmers Market. One holds that after they opened their restaurant, the Magee family asked to have tables and chairs installed so their customers could dine in comfort. The other, courtesy of Fred Beck, holds that a woman purchased a sandwich for lunch and grabbed a nearby orange crate to sit upon. She then punctured her hindquarters on a protruding nail. According to Beck, the woman sought out Roger Dahlhjelm and held him personally responsible for her injury. In response, Dahlhjelm ordered a few tables and chairs scattered around the Market; to make the experience even more pleasant, he also ordered a few umbrellas. One way or the other, dining on the Market's patios became an integral part of the experience.

Magee's Nuts was one of two nut shops at Farmers Market during its earliest years. The other, Magic Nuts, eventually became Ultimate Nut and Candy, and both have been operating continuously at the Farmers Market ever since. The Magee family typically organized two floats for Fall Festival parades, one celebrating the nut shop, the other their famous Irish cuisine at Magee's Kitchen.

While grocery, produce, and restaurants were mainstays at Farmers Market, other shops found the atmosphere—and the steady flow of customers—to their liking as well. A wine merchant, offering private label "Paul Jones" bottles, helped complete the total grocery shopping experience that area residents cherished. They found that, from soup to nuts, they could do all their grocery shopping at the Farmers Market.

The Fall Festival parade at Farmers Market became a surprisingly successful promotion. Over the years, Roger Dahlhjelm and Fred Beck tinkered with the concept, adding automobiles to lead the parade with Dahlhjelm in the most prominent seat. Beck secured marching bands and, at least once, an elephant to participate. The parade grew so popular that Beck had temporary bleachers installed along the route to accommodate the spectators.

This Mesulam's Burbank Farms parade float typifies the whimsical attitude of the affair, celebrating the longevity that flowed directly from consuming Burbank produce. The float is intriguing for another feature—it uses the older, original Farmers Public Market name although, by the time this photograph was taken, the Market had stopped using that extra word in its promotional material and the city no longer used it at all.

Fred Beck was relentless in his promotion of Farmers Market. It was his idea to recruit merchants (including Bedig's, shown here) to create zany outfits and floats in order to generate silly—and therefore newsworthy—images to promote the place. He also recruited a circus to the property, organized dining events, arranged for starlets to be photographed at the Market, and publicized every quirk he could find. After the early, lean years, Beck eventually had sufficient funds to purchase space in the *Los Angeles Times*. He created a daily column, always on page two, which promoted the place, shared outrageous stories (some fanciful, some not), and, on occasion, warned shoppers away from fruit not up to standard or vegetables delivered too early to be quite ripe. The column became one of the most popular features in the paper, second only to *Dick Tracy*.

Roger Dahlhjelm occasionally came up with promotional gimmicks to publicize Farmers Market. Dahlhjelm once organized a Boy's Band. He recruited local lads to participate, providing instruments and a conductor. He built a full-scale band shell in the middle of the Market's parking lot. Nobody complained about the absence of females, but someone eventually chided the Farmers Market for "exploiting" youngsters. Dahlhjelm, a somewhat prickly fellow, took offense and promptly disbanded his band.

This photograph shows a persona only Fred Beck could have created. "Chef Baloni" reflected Beck's love of food and drink and his remarkably expressive face. Chef Baloni wandered the aisles of the Farmers Market, offering free recipes and cooking advice. At one point, Roger Dahlhjelm gave Beck an "office" inside the Market to make Beck another Market "attraction." Once Beck discovered small children gawking at him, he quit the office quickly.

Three

ROAR WITH GILMORE

The history of Farmers Market is inextricably tied to the history of the Gilmore Oil Company. From the turn of the 20th century, when oil was first discovered on the Gilmore dairy farm, through the mid-1940s, Gilmore Oil Company was at the core of the family's business.

Gilmore Oil was central to the very existence of Farmers Market. It provided the financial base that enabled Earl Bell Gilmore to take a chance on the idea of Farmers Market. It was a promotional partner to the Farmers Market, most notably in the marriage of Gilmore Stadium, a facility next door to the Market designed primarily—although not quite exclusively—to promote Gilmore gas. Gilmore Oil was a primary source of fuel on the West Coast, and thus it provided the power that drove the cars that enabled customers to get to and from the Market and enabled the farmers who first sold produce to those customers to transport their goods to the corner of Third Street and Fairfax Avenue.

Perhaps most critically, the spirit and energy that E. B. Gilmore and his Gilmore Oil team brought to their enterprise informed and infused the approach that, even today, drives business to the Farmers Market. Gilmore Oil Company used all the tools at their disposal to promote their products—clever advertisements, radio programs, an extraordinary array of stunts and publicity initiatives, icons, and the creation of household phrases. E. B. used all these to generate attention. The attention led to commercial success and, with his Market partners Roger Dahlhjelm and Fred Beck, E. B. Gilmore brought that same spirit—and the same measure of success—to Farmers Market.

Had the western United States not been invited to "Roar with Gilmore," it seems unlikely that anyone would have invited friends and family to "Meet me at Third and Fairfax."

In the late 1880s, Arthur Fremont Gilmore started drilling water wells in order to expand his dairy herd. He found oil. In a matter of years, the dairy farm at Third Street and Fairfax Avenue had vanished completely, replaced by a vast, highly productive oil field. This 1914 photograph shows the oil field, already providing jobs for a crew of workers who extracted the rich oil from the land.

In its earliest stages, the oil company produced petroleum products used as machinery lubricants and paving material. The headquarters, on the former dairy farm property, retained only the agrarian look; everything else associated with the family business changed completely. As the signage here indicates, the company was known as the A. F. Gilmore Oil Company; the initials were later dropped in favor of the simpler Gilmore Oil Company.

As cars and planes became common sights, E. B. Gilmore assumed leadership of the family business. To promote Gilmore Blu-Green gas and Red Lion gas, he adopted the slogan "Roar with Gilmore," and then he hired a barnstorming pilot named Roscoe Turner to fly a Gilmore-powered plane around the West, a rather bold concept in its own right. But E. B. was not done. He agreed to put Turner's lion cub in the cockpit with Turner. Gilmore the lion cub became instant stars. When the dashing Turner landed on airport runways, dirt landing strips, and even open fields, large crowds flocked to see the lion cub that could fly. When they saw the cub, they also saw Gilmore Oil logos and brand names on the plane. The two set air-speed records and, over time, they logged tens of thousands of miles. They also generated so much publicity that none could miss it. When Louis B. Mayer wanted a symbol to announce that audiences were about to see an MGM movie, he inserted a roaring lion. It is believed that the choice was inspired by Gilmore's roaring success.

At some point early on during the campaign, Roscoe Turner and Gilmore drew the attention of the SPCA (Society for the Prevention of Cruelty to Animals), which expressed concern about the cub's safety. E. B. Gilmore addressed the problem quickly and with his usual flair—he outfitted the cub with a parachute and a leather flying cap. The resulting images only enhanced the cub's celebrity and expanded the number of publicity shots the cub generated wherever he went.

Even beyond its promotional cache, speed fascinated E. B. Gilmore. He sponsored John Cobb in the Gilmore-fueled Railton Red Lion, a sleek silver spaceship on wheels that, running on the salt flats at Bonneville in Utah, established a land speed record of 369.7 miles per hour. The record stood for seven years.

E. B. Gilmore sponsored racers at Indianapolis, including cars driven by Stubby Stubblefield and Rex Mays. Famed driver Wilbur Shaw, shown here (left) with the Shaw Gilmore Special and the equally famous Gilmore (center), won at Indy in 1937. Eventually Shaw would win three Indy 500s. His victories followed Kelly Petillo's 1935 Indy victory in the "Gilmore Speedway Special."

All Gilmore gas promotions had but a single goal—selling Gilmore products. Gas was available at a network of more than a 1,100 stations, including this one at the corner of Wilshire Boulevard and La Brea Avenue in Los Angeles, just a few blocks from Farmers Market. Customers at many Gilmore stations purchased gas from pumps that featured glass in which they could see the gas flowing to their tanks.

This is a typical Gilmore gas station from the era when they were ubiquitous on the West Coast. The tanker truck is typical as well, featuring the Gilmore logos. Most of the stations and the trucks used the same color scheme, which appeared on Gilmore racing vehicles and promotional airplanes—a combination of cream and red that was typically presented in a swooping, stylish fashion connoting speed and power.

In the late 1940s, Gilmore Oil was merged with the future Mobil Oil Company, and E. B. Gilmore built a huge gas station on Beverly Boulevard near Farmers Market. Offering customers a nickel per gallon savings for pumping their own gas, E. B. called his concept a "gas-a-teria." It was the first dedicated self-serve gas station; so unique that *Life* magazine featured it in a two-page photographic spread.

This is a promotional photograph for a typical Gilmore gas station. The attendant is working through a service checklist. In the era of Gilmore stations, service was an integral part of the routine, as were uniforms. Customers expected Gilmore service to include an oil check, full service as needed, and a clean windshield, too. (Photograph by Dick Whittington.)

A contingent of Gilmore station attendants provides service at another typical Gilmore outlet. The sign in the background, featuring the classic Gilmore lion head icon, was common to most Gilmore stations. There were more than 1,100 Gilmore gas stations in total, from Washington to the Southern California border, and they varied in size from two-pump operations to full-service facilities such as this one. Gilmore Oil products were available at more than 3,500 locations. (Photograph by Dick Whittington.)

In addition to his sojourns with copilot Gilmore, Roscoe Turner, who was known to be something of a ladies man, occasionally hosted airborne tea parties to generate even more publicity for the company. He also shuttled people around the West; here he is seen (at right) with guests at the Del Coronado Hotel near San Diego.

Many of Roscoe Turner's flights were undertaken at the direction of E. B. Gilmore, who often arranged for friends and dignitaries to be flown to and fro in one of the company's stable of airplanes. E. B. is seen here (at left) with a friend while Turner (in the cockpit) awaits boarding and clearance for take-off. (Photograph by Irving Lippman.)

E. B. invented the Gilmore Endurance Run, a demonstration in which he would test a vehicle directly from a showroom floor (in this case, a Hudson) on Muroc Dry Lake in California. The concept, which let Gilmore Economy Runs, tested standard cars for mileage, endurance, and performance. It was the precursor to stock car races.

Pilot Earl Ortman flew a Gilmore-sponsored aircraft, the "Gilmore Record Breaker," from Canada to Mexico in a record-setting time. The 1935 flight took just over five and a half hours from border to border. These "stunts" reflected E. B. Gilmore's consuming fascination with speed; he also sponsored the nation's premiere speedboat racer of the time, Ward Angilley.

E. B. Gilmore's sponsorship of countless vehicles, from midget racers to speedboats to planes to race cars, gave him the opportunity to witness the fruits of his work. Here he is seen in the cockpit of the Railton Red Lion at Bonneville in Utah. There is no evidence to suggest that he actually drove the car—the fastest land vehicle of its day—but he was usually present for its runs and always at hand when Gilmore Oil products were being demonstrated or powering his many projects.

This Bonneville racetrack photograph shows the Railton Lion at speed. E. B. Gilmore was a pioneer in the marriage of speed sports to marketing. For his participation in everything from land speed record attempts to Indianapolis 500 sponsorships to his devotion to midget racing, E. B. Gilmore was eventually honored in many museums and motor sport centers, including the Indianapolis Motor Speedway Hall of Fame and the Sprint Car Hall of Fame.

The Gilmore Oil Company's promotional efforts took full advantage of star power. The legendary Amelia Earhart was among the many celebrities who came to be associated with Gilmore products, as in this photograph of the aviatrix with a Gilmore plane. In a similar promotion, Gilmore arranged for a Gilmore aircraft to fly Loretta Young to Boulder Dam for a promotional photo shoot.

E. B. Gilmore was never shy about making his planes available in circumstances where a photograph might result. In this shot, Roscoe Turner (with aviator cap on) is about to provide air transport for the governor of California, James "Sunny Jim" Rolfe (to the right of Turner). The governor and Gilmore were friends, and E. B. often made aircraft available for junkets around the state. (Photograph by Henzel Photography.)

Gilmore gas stations could be found up and down the West Coast, in cities and on rural byways. This station, in Portland, Oregon, featured a unique attraction. That enormous gas pump almost certainly did not dispense Blu-Green gas, but it was an arresting means of drawing customers as they motored by.

His exposure was so extensive and his storied copiloting adventures so captivating that Gilmore the lion cub eventually drew crowds even when he was not wearing his parachute and leather cap. At this local Gilmore gas station promotion, Gilmore is on display in a cage, drawing a substantial crowd without his companion Roscoe Turner or an airplane.

This stylish and sleek car was part of the Gilmore stable. Dubbed "The Topper Car" after the popular ghost movie star of the moment, the vehicle was used in parades and on road trips, including this one to the Los Angeles Harbor in San Pedro to generate attention for Gilmore products. Those are loudspeakers mounted on the front fenders of the car, an accessory that made it possible for passengers to talk to parade spectators or for the driver to broadcast the merits of using Gilmore Oil products. The entire spectrum of Gilmore Oil equipment and products, from the glass globes atop Gilmore pumps to signage and cans of Head Lion oil, are today coveted by petroleum industry collectors. Bidding for some items can be furious and expensive (a collector recently purchased a neon Gilmore sign for several thousand dollars). The Topper Car is among the cherished Gilmore prizes—it is currently held in the Petersen Automotive Museum's Los Angeles collection.

Of all the extensive promotional efforts the Gilmore Oil Company launched, few were more popular or recognized than the Gilmore Radio Circus, a radio program sponsored by and promoting Gilmore products. Even Gilmore the lion made appearances on the program, seen here giving one of the show's cast members the once-over. The program created what became the longest advertising jingle in history, the Gilmore gas song. Each week, listeners were invited to submit a new verse to the song and each winner was added to the jingle. In addition to becoming lyricists, the winners also received prizes from the Gilmore product line. Here is a typical winning verse, submitted by Micky Lorange of Los Angeles: "The night was cold and rainy / The streets were wet and slick / The Chevy old and rusty / But, oh boy, it had some kick! / We dashed past many Packards, / And their owners said "Some class!" / What makes that boat so speedy? / And we hollered, "Blu-Green Gas!"

E. B. Gilmore was never far from any effort to promote Gilmore products. He even made billboard appearances, assuring customers of the value of the line. His association with motor sports, speed records, and the many other publicity efforts of the company made him as much a part of the company's brand as Blu-Green gas.

Roscoe Turner provided the ride when actress Loretta Young took a publicity trip to Boulder Dam near Las Vegas. The junket may have been in support of the public works project then under construction or to promote a movie, but the result was a series of photographs that made their way into newspapers and magazines—and elevated the Gilmore Oil Company profile in the process.

Kelly Petillo drove the Gilmore Speedway Racer to victory in the 1935 Indianapolis 500, the first of two Gilmore victories in that race. This particular victory also generated a record when Petillo captured the checkered flag at an average speed of 106.24 miles per hour. While unimpressive in the context of contemporary speeds in the Indy race, that record was quite a feat in its day. Over time, E. B. Gilmore sponsored dozens of record-setting efforts. He and the company held land-speed records at Bonneville, air-speed records between countless western cities, and time/distance records from every U.S. border—the air-speed record from Canada to Mexico and, very briefly, a New York-to-Los Angeles record as well. Seen here are Petillo (right) and Jimmy Dunham, a local mechanic who worked with Petillo.

To serve sportsmen who loved the open West, the Gilmore Oil Company published an extensive series of fishing and hunting guides, available only at Gilmore gas stations. The guides were authentic; research was conducted in person and the company created a Fish and Game Scout Car to demonstrate its commitment to the guides it offered.

When local regulations banned derricks and refining in residential areas, the Gilmore Oil Company removed its assets from the land where Farmers Market would eventually rise. Among other facilities, they owned and operated this refinery in Los Angeles on Twenty-eighth Street. The Gilmore oil truck at the facility was a common sight in the West.

The remarkable history of the Gilmore Oil Company is celebrated at Farmers Market's Gilmore Heritage Auto Show. Late night host Jay Leno arrived for the inaugural show in a rare antique from his collection, a wooden-bodied Rolls Royce. The vehicle overheated as the star pulled onto the property and Farmers Market staff came to his rescue, lying sawdust to absorb the spillage and providing water to fill the radiator.

Los Angeles mayor Richard Riordan (left) inaugurated the first Gilmore Heritage Auto Show in 1994. He joined A. F. Gilmore Company president Hank Hilty (right) for the show and presented a Mayor's Award to his selection for the best car in the show. The Gilmore Auto Show is now a fixture in the Market's calendar, annually drawing car collectors and fans on the first Saturday in June.

Four

THERE USED TO BE

A BALLPARK

Farmers Market enjoyed enormous popularity and success from the day it opened in 1934, but it was the only attraction on the land once known as "Gilmore Island." Indeed, the A. F. Gilmore property has always surrounded the Farmers Market with other venues, all designed to create a more fun-filled experience and smart marketing synergy.

Those who came to the property to see a race at Gilmore Stadium were a short stroll away from Farmers Market. Those who attended a baseball game at Gilmore Field could have lunch or dinner at the Market, just next door. Audiences arriving to see a Gilmore Drive-In movie or a show at Pan Pacific Auditorium were close enough to enjoy a snack or some shopping. Gilmore Bank customers could walk from the tellers to a toffee shop. Consumers shopping at the Dell were on the north side of the Market's parking lot.

These venues have a history all their own, yet each is part of the Farmers Market's heritage as well. Many who cherish the Market today attribute their initial affection to the other attractions that first drew them to the property.

The venues overlapped one another. Gilmore Stadium opened just a few weeks before Farmers Market made its debut; Gilmore Field followed the stadium but remained on the property slightly longer. The Gilmore Drive-In had the greatest longevity of all the other venues on Gilmore land, surviving into the 1977. Gilmore Bank opened in the 1950s and, in a new location, remains part of the Farmers Market experience today.

Each of these storied venues has its own history and its own unique character, yet all are, ultimately, part of the Farmers Market experience.

Screen Actors Guild

★

FIRST ANNUAL
FILM STARS
... FROLIC ...

★

GILMORE STADIUM
Fairfax at Beverly ... Los Angeles

... Price 5ᶜ

Gilmore Stadium opened in May 1934 just north of the site where Farmers Market would open two months later. The stadium's first event celebrated the arts; it was staged by the Screen Actors Guild and hosted by its president, Eddie Cantor. The event was a bit removed for the "real" purpose of the stadium, yet it was fitting, for Hollywood and Farmers Market were just about to become great friends.

Earl B. Gilmore, Builder of the stadium dedicated by the Screen Actors Guild.

FOR BENEFIT OF OUTDOOR SPORTS

★ ★ ★

*Y*OU ARE celebrating with us today an achievement ... the completion and dedication of Southern California's newest stadium ... which has been built primarily for the advancement of recreation and outdoor sports. ℂ This amphitheatre fulfills a long-felt need for such facilities in this community. The centralized location is ideal ... for the city, in a progressive development, has built up around it. Here clean, well managed sport events, civic festivals and theatricals will be staged. Here every precaution is taken to assure the comfort and pleasure of patrons. ℂ We know you will enjoy your first visit here ... and we sincerely hope many another happy hour will be yours in this stadium.

Earl B. Gilmore

On the back cover of the SAG program, E. B. Gilmore welcomed one and all as he dedicated his new stadium. He offered entertainment, fun, and a hearty welcome. The facility would quickly become a venue with appeal to broad audiences seeking the many and richly varied events E. B. promised them.

The second event at Gilmore Stadium, in May 1934, featured motorcycle races. The facility had seating for 18,000, with the seats in an oval configuration that completely enclosed the track. While the stadium was well suited to races featuring motorcycles, it also proved to be quite versatile, with ample space for wide and eclectic events like circuses and rodeos.

Gilmore Stadium was built for midget racing. The format was brand new in 1934—only a handful of the tiny one-seat racers existed. E. B. Gilmore commissioned famed auto engineer Fred Offenhauser, and their collaboration created the engine that became the standard for midgets; it easily reached 100 miles per hour. Bob Swanson is seen here with a midget racer; Swanson won more races at Gilmore Stadium than any other driver.

Midget racing at Gilmore Stadium took place in a season that ran from May to "Tanksgiving." The rapid little racers spun around the track on a surface of clay and decomposed granite, specifically created to be slippery enough to allow the cars to slide on curves but stable enough to prevent dust from rising from the surface to obscure drivers' views or coat the crowds assembled to see the races.

There were both day and night midget races at Gilmore Stadium. Drivers were literally packed into their little cars—there was barely room for a single seat and the cockpit was very close. It was also wide open; drivers' upper bodies rose above the lines of the cars and, while they wore helmets, accidents were a source of genuine danger. Four drivers lost their lives racing at Gilmore Stadium.

This is without doubt the most famous photograph ever taken at Gilmore Stadium. The driver of the car in flames, Fred Friday, managed to navigate his way to the infield of the stadium and escape safely, but the image that resulted was so dramatic that it made its way around the world rapidly. Car buffs worldwide, especially those intrigued by customizing the look of their own personal vehicles, were so enraptured by the image of a racer flying around a track in flames that they immediately adopted the look—if not the reality—of it. Soon hot rods all over America were motoring around their hometowns with flames painted on the front fenders. The prospect of witnessing such events made the midget race programs at Gilmore Stadium so popular that the stadium became a center of the sport. It also provided a solid foundation upon which other events could be booked and, once the stadium had established its reputation as a leading midget venue, it began to expand its offerings.

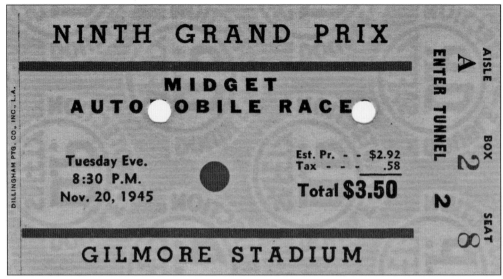

NINTH GRAND PRIX

MIDGET
AUTOMOBILE RACE

Tuesday Eve.
8:30 P.M.
Nov. 20, 1945

Est. Pr. - - $2.92
Tax - - - .58

Total $3.50

GILMORE STADIUM

This is a ticket stub from a Gilmore Stadium midget car race. On a couple of occasions, the stadium actually drew audiences beyond its seating capacity. The popularity of the little racers generated fans with fierce allegiances to one driver or another. Long after the stadium closed and midgets stopped racing there, fans would gather for an annual tribute to midget racers and the men who drove them—often the annual celebration took place on the grounds of the Gilmore Adobe.

Gilmore Stadium was equally suitable for football as it was for midget racing. The first professional football team in Los Angeles, the Bulldogs, played their home games on the grass field that sat inside the track where the midget cars raced. Football proved a popular draw and those who came to see a game often walked the short distance from the stadium to Farmers Market to eat or shop. (Photograph by Carroll Photo Service.)

Loyola University's varsity football team played their home games at Gilmore Stadium. NFL players in All-Star games also played there, giving fans a chance to see its East Coast stars play. It also hosted college All-Star games, including one featuring a local star, USC's John Ferraro, who later became president of the Los Angeles City Council representing the district that included Farmers Market.

ALL AMERICANS

FOOTBALL

EASTERN COLLEGE STARS
Featuring: "CHARLEY" CONERLY — "SKIPPY" MINISI — "LEN" FORD — "BOB" MANN

VS

WESTERN COLLEGE STARS
Featuring: "BOBBY" LAYNE — "JOHNNY" FERRARO — "TOMMY" FEARS — "JOE" PERRY

SUNDAY AFTERNOON JANUARY THE 18th 1948
KICKOFF — 2 P.M.
GILMORE STADIUM
BEVERLY AT FAIRFAX
RESERVATIONS — STADIUM BOX OFFICE — WHITNEY 1163

As part of his 1948 campaign, Pres. Harry Truman spoke at a rally held at Gilmore Stadium. He addressed the pressures and crosscurrents of the cold war and the dangers it presented to the United States. In a typically blunt—and frequently quoted—turn of phrase, Truman urged his audience to "keep a stiff upper lip."

SUNSET RANCH

Presents

KEN MAYNARD

Stuart Hamblen ★ **Betty Goodan** ★ **Jimmy Wakely**

10¢

10¢

⁕ RODEO ⁕

MARCH 28, 1943

GILMORE STADIUM

Cowboy Ken Maynard brought his rodeo to Gilmore Stadium. It was a complete show, offering audiences traditional rodeo events such as bull riding and bronco busting. These events were typically set up, presented, and broken down over the course of a single day or a weekend. The ticket price for this show, one dime, is one of the reasons Greater Los Angeles called Gilmore the "workingman's stadium."

Gilmore Stadium featured such a varied collection of offerings that it frequently published entertainment guides to provide visitors a full lineup. This 1934 guide lists a host of scheduled events and suggests that the aim of those managing the facility was to reach an audience as broad and as varied as possible.

Ticket Prices

MOTORCYCLE AND MIDGET AUTOMOBILE RACES

General Admission	$ .40
Reserve Seats (Including tax)	.60
Box Seats (Including tax)	.75
Children (15 years)	.15

PROFESSIONAL FOOTBALL

General Admission	.75
Reserve Seats	1.10
Box Seats	1.65
Members of "Gate Crashers" Club	.25

LOYOLA FOOTBALL GAMES

General Admission	1.10
Reserve Seats	1.65
Box Seats	1.65

CUMNOCK FOOTBALL GAMES

General Admission	.40
Box Seats	.75
Children (15 years)	.15

How to reach the Stadium

BY BUS—Take Beverly Bus on Hill Street from Tenth to Second Streets; On Second to Beverly Boulevard and on Beverly going West. All Los Angeles Railway Busses and Cars transfer to Beverly Boulevard Bus.

BY AUTOMOBILE—Drive to corner of Beverly Boulevard and Fairfax Avenue. Beverly Boulevard is one-half mile North of Wilshire Boulevard. Fairfax is three miles West of Western Avenue.

What's? Doing!

at

GILMORE STADIUM

While midget racing dominated the automotive entertainment at Gilmore Stadium, it was often supplemented with other forms of car racing. This flyer for the uniquely spelled "Jolopy" stampede invited spectators to witness what would, in the future, be known as a demolition derby, an event in which the last car running—and still mobile—wins the race.

America's Greatest Thrill Show
A NEVER TO BE FORGOTTEN EVENT

JOLOPY
Stampede

Twenty Thousand Thrill Mad Fans Will Crowd the Beautiful Stadium for this Stupendous Specta-drama

GILMORE STADIUM
SATURDAY EVENING, 8:30 P.M.
JULY 27, 1935

How many times have you experienced the thrill of Horse Races, Auto Races, Dog Races, Football, Baseball, Polo, etc. We now present America's latest sensation, the "JOLOPY STAMPEDE," in this mammoth show each spectator becomes part of a huge **thrill event** creating a three hour program of entertainment which you will never forget. Many unparalleled acts blended into one huge attraction. **Laughs and Nerve Tingles** from start to finish. Attend this, the first introductory "Jolopy Stampede" ever held.

Fifty Beautiful Automobiles will be **given away** during the performance. You may be **fortunate** and drive one home when the curtain is rung down on this **thrill** of thrillers. Cars of the following makes: Dodge, Cadillac, Packard, Lincoln, Chevrolet, Ford, Hudson, Willys, Hupmobile, La Salle, Buick, Plymouth, Chrysler, Lafayette, Nash, Pontiac, Oldsmobile, Reo and many others. **50 in all**—1928 to 1935 vintage—every one a car to be proud of. **No drawing of tickets**—but what a surprise. What a **sensation**, you cannot afford to miss it. Tickets now on sale at **3000 Independent service stations** throughout **Southern California**. Get yours while they last. Be one of the first **twenty-thousand** participators in the thriller of all times, the "JOLOPY STAMPEDE".

The Date **Saturday Evening, July, 27th.**
The Time **8:30 P. M.**
The Place **Gilmore Stadium.**
The Attraction the **JOLOPY STAMPEDE.**
The Price **$1.00; Tax 10c; Total, $1.10.**

Commonwealth Press

Los Angeles County

WOMEN'S AUTOMOBILE DRIVING TOURNAMENT

Presenting

"TRAFFIC AUTO DRIVING CLASSICS"

Conducted
By
Col. Arthur B. Hickox
"Wild Bill"

Veteran Automobile
Racing Driver

—— Referee ——

GILMORE STADIUM ... SUNDAY ... OCTOBER 27th ... Starting 2:00 P.M. Sharp
Sponsored by Co-operative Automotive Group

GLENN E. SHAW, Contest Manager

Official Headquarters
1420 NORTH WILCOX AVE.
Telephone GLadstone 5837

Another motor sport event offered at Gilmore Stadium was this one, which featured women participating in races that, at the time and certainly at the stadium, were almost exclusively the domain of men. This event may have had extra appeal to the housewives who used Farmers Market for their grocery shopping—it was certainly another attempt to draw new audiences to the stadium and to the Market next door.

In 1939, Hollywood entertainers again returned to Gilmore Stadium, following the inaugural SAG celebration in 1934. This time, the performers were stuntmen who created an entire show of their daring, although most carefully planned and executed, exploits. Faux fights, pratfalls, car chases, and other movie stunts were featured, providing the seldom-recognized stunt performers an audience that usually did not see them except in disguise.

Boxing matches were booked at Gilmore Stadium frequently. This program for an "All Star Sporting Club Boxing Carnival" offered fight fans a full card of bouts in several weight divisions. It also featured an image of Gilmore Stadium, which provides a full view of its configuration and interior layout.

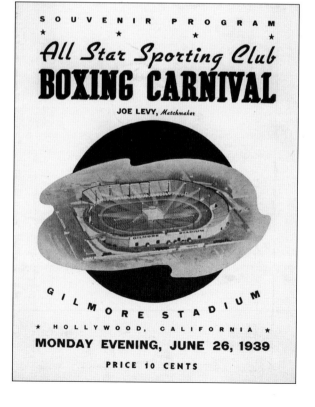

There were several major fights staged at Gilmore Stadium, including a middleweight championship contest in which two well-known and talented fighters of the era fought before a capacity house and, via radio, a national audience. Events of this magnitude, as well as the stadium's staple midget car racing, helped establish Gilmore Stadium as a national sports venue.

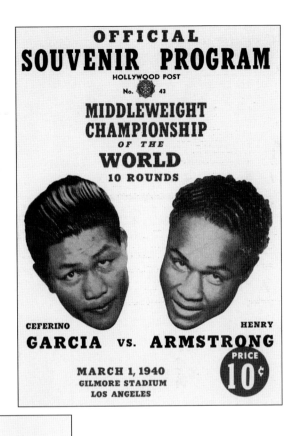

PROGRAM OF EVENTS
★

DIRECTORS
ALBERT S. ROGELL LEW LANDERS JOS. A. McDONOUGH
EDWARD A. SUTHERLAND LEROY PRINZ VERNON KEAYS

MASTERS OF CEREMONIES
KEN MURRAY MILTON BERLE GUS MACK

JUDGES
ABBOTT & COSTELLO WALLACE FORD MERLE OBERON NANCY KELLY
BILLY GILBERT JOHN GARFIELD MAUREEN O'HARA ROSEMARY LANE
BUCK JONES PORTER HALL ERROL FLYNN ADOLPHE MENJOU
MISCHA AUER JEAN HERSHOLT LINDA DARNELL LLOYD NOLAN
ROSALIND RUSSELL MARY LIVINGSTONE JOHN PAYNE WILLIAM GARGAN
RUDY VALEE RALPH MORGAN LYNN BARI TEX RITTER
EDWARD ARNOLD ROY ROGERS ROBERT PRESTON DONALD BARRY

1. **PARADE OF PARTICIPANTS**
   David J. Malloy, Director
2. **ATHLETIC EVENTS**
   Sanctioned by A.A.U.
   a. 880-yard Run
   b. 100-yard Open
   c. 50-yard Dash (Women)
   d. One Mile Race
   e. 120-yard Low Hurdle
   f. High Jump
3. **MOTOR SCOOTER RACE**
   Frank Cooper, Director
4. **CALIFORNIA GIRLS' TROOP**
   Dr. Leonard Stallcup, Director
5. **BICYCLE RACE**
   Philip Mole, Musty Crebs, and
   Hans Ohrt, Directors
6. **STEEPLECHASE**
7. **MOTOR SCOOTER POLO**
8. **ESKIMO DOG SLED RACE**
9. **DON STEWART**
   Juvenile Champion

10. **HORSE RACE—3/5 MILE**
    "Malicious"
11. **VICTOR McLAGLEN'S MOTOR-
    CYCLE CORPS**
12. **NOAH'S ARK HANDICAP**
13. **RUSSIAN COSSACKS**
    Mischa Auer, Director
14. **PONY EXPRESS RACE**
    Buck Jones, Director
15. **VICTOR McLAGLEN'S GIRL
    TROUPE**
    Capt. George Henning, Director
16. **CAMEL RACE**
17. **GREYHOUND RACE**
18. **MOVIE COWBOY RACE**
    Tex Ritter, Donald Barry, Bill Elliot,
    Brad King, Russell Hayden, Bob Steele,
    George Houston
19. **HAP RUGGLES**
    Death Defying Ride
20. **FINALE**

GREETINGS FROM
Young's Market Company

An unusual Gilmore Stadium event featured camel races and dog-sled contests. Milton Berle and Abbott and Costello joined the festivities. In 1934, Lou Costello was down on his luck, living in a baseball field shed on the Gilmore property and sleeping on piled-up bases. He awoke one day to find farmers all over the place. He bought a pickle, his meal for the day—or so Fred Beck reported.

WATER FOLLIES of 1944

85 STARS **25 ACTS** **36 MERMAIDS**

Great Combination
of Water and Stage Show

STARRING

BUSTER CRABBE

Swim and Screen Star
Olympic Champion

Show takes place in
$25,000 Portable
Stage and Pools

Now Playing
Nightly at 8:30

★

MATINEES SUNDAYS
AND JULY 4th

★

DON'T MISS IT!

★

Tickets Now on Sale in Advance at Southern
Calif. Music Co., 737 S. Hill St., Hollywood
Music Shop, 6634 Hollywood Blvd., All
Mutual Agencies and at Gilmore Stadium
Office, Beverly at Fairfax. WHitney 1163.

FEATURING ★

★

FAMOUS HOPKIN TWINS
Stars of both World's Aquacades

★

FRANK FOSTER
Great Water Comedian

★

FOUR "DILLY-DALLIES"
Funny Water Comedians,
Starred and Featured at N. Y. Aquacade

★

JOE PETERSON
Daredevil of the Spring Board

★

ALF PHILLIPS
Canada's Diving Champion at Olympics

★

WHITEY HART
Acrobatic Wonder of the Diving Boards

★

36 BALLET
SWIMMING DOLLS
Rhythm — Precision — Grace
and Skill

★

MISS "CORKY" GILLESEN
Olympic Lady Diving Champion

★

THE THREE KINGS
Sensational Balancing Act

★

MARION ROBERGE
The 1944 Singing Sensation

★

Different Than Other Shows

WORLD'S GREATEST MUSICAL **REVUE IN WATER**

GILMORE STADIUM

BEVERLY BOULEVARD at FAIRFAX

In 1944, Hollywood star Buster Crabbe came to Gilmore Stadium with his Water Follies show. The event required the temporary construction of a full-sized swimming pool, large enough for the show and deep enough to accommodate divers. Creating whatever suitable equipment each event required inside the stadium, staging the event, and the dismantling whatever had been constructed was a regular part of the stadium's life. Whether for boxing matches, political rallies, or rodeos, the stadium was suitably flexible and compact to allow for these amenities yet large enough to draw crowds sufficient to justify the expense. Gilmore Stadium and Farmers Market lore have long held that a similar program, featuring the enormously popular Esther Williams, also took place at the stadium under similar circumstances—a pool constructed and dismantled in a matter of days—but the A. F. Gilmore archives have no record of the Williams event.

Even local Boy Scouts took advantage of the expansive field inside Gilmore Stadium. Hundreds of area scouts staged a jamboree on the grass interior of the facility. In this instance, Hollywood got in on the act once more as the most famous cartoon rabbit on earth joined the scouts around a campfire to roast his favorite dish.

1947
SCOUT
CIRCUS

©WARNER BROS. CARTOONS

Los Angeles Area Council
BOY SCOUTS OF AMERICA
Gilmore Stadium — MAY 2-3
Program Compliments May Co. Boy Scout Trading Post

Before America entered the Second World War, there was a sustained campaign to provide aid and comfort to those in England suffering from steady air attacks. Gilmore Stadium lent its support to that effort, displaying a German Messerschmitt fighter that had been downed over Great Britain. The proceeds from the event were donated to the victims of the assault England was enduring at the time. (Photograph by Carroll Photo Service.)

This aerial view of Gilmore Stadium shows the reasonably good-sized seating capacity as well as its slightly banked clay and decomposed granite track and the sizable infield on which non-auto racing events were staged. The stadium was close enough to Farmers Market that its restrooms were available to customers in the early days.

Sixteen years after it opened, Gilmore Stadium was razed under the supervision of its manager, Gene Doyle. By 1950, professional sports had moved west, smaller stadiums were less economically viable, and E. B. Gilmore had found a more attractive use for the land (see chapter 4). It had given L.A. lots of entertainment while it served as a valuable partner to Farmers Market and a promotional tool for Gilmore Oil Company.

In 1938, the A. F. Gilmore Company began construction on a professional baseball facility, Gilmore Field. It was built for a Pacific Coast League team. The team's ownership was hardly typical—the owners included Cecile B. DeMille, Barbara Stanwyck, and Bing Crosby. In their first year, the Hollywood Stars shared L.A.'s Wrigley Field with the town's other PCL team, the Angels, but they needed a home of their own. E. B. Gilmore built it for them. Gilmore Field was sited north and east of Farmers Market and due east of Gilmore Stadium. It was an intimate, decidedly fan-friendly structure, precisely the sort of stadium that some 60 years later teams in San Francisco, Baltimore, and St. Louis would seek to emulate. From the day it opened, fans called the place "friendly Gilmore Field."

Gilmore Field was modern and inviting. The patio-like entrance had ample room for pregame groups to gather, and the smaller structures just outside the gates enabled fans to buy tickets on the spot or pick them up at a will call window. Fans shared the sizable parking lot with visitors to Farmers Market. It was common for those fans to dine at the Market before or after each game.

Inside, Gilmore Field was so intimate that fans sitting in the bleachers regularly engaged the players in conversation; they also shared the occasional beer with outfielders, too. The ballpark seated 14,000 and people sat as close to the field as possible—home plate was 34 feet from the first row of seats, while first and third bases were only 24 feet. (Photograph by Mott Studios.)

There has surely never been an opening day quite like that which greeted the Hollywood Stars on May 2, 1939. In addition to the celebrity owners of the club, the crowd included Jack Benny, Gary Cooper, Robert Taylor, and Gail Patrick. Renowned L.A. restaurateur Bob Cobb, the inventor of Cobb Salad, delivered the ceremonial first pitch. His catcher was Joe E. Brown. The opening-day crowd probably exceeded the ballyard's maximum seating, and tickets, if they could be found, were sold at premium prices. The Hollywood Stars played the Seattle Rainiers, but the packed house was probably just as eager to see all the luminaries as they were to watch a baseball game. Over the years, the team would comport itself reasonably well on the field, but their close connection to Hollywood caused considerable derision among local sportswriters, who dubbed the team the "Twinks" as soon as they took to their new facility.

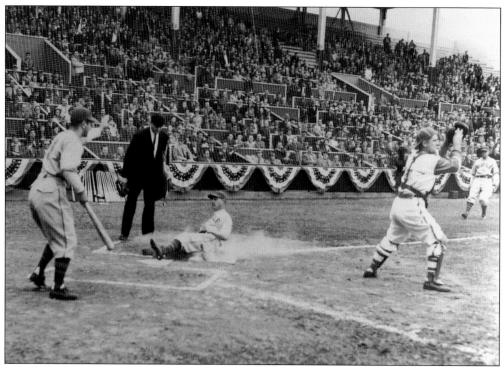

Jo Jo White of the Rainiers slides into home plate during action on opening day at Gilmore Field. He was safe at the plate, contributing to a total of eight runs for the Seattle club against the Stars' five. That the Stars lost their inaugural game did not seem to bother the fans at all—they had come to pass judgment on the new ballpark and to see all those "real" Hollywood stars.

After Bob Cobb threw out the ceremonial first pitch on opening day at Gilmore Field, he was replaced on the mound by Jane Wyman. She tossed a second pitch to Joe E. Brown as her fans in the stands and on the field cheered her effort.

Although the lighting conditions inside the park were considerably less effective than modern-day systems, the Hollywood Stars nonetheless played many night games. The entrance to the ballpark promoted the home team on its marquee. At any given game, fans were likely to encounter all sorts of stars. George Burns and Gracie Allen attended games frequently, as did singer Tony Martin.

The scoreboard at Gilmore Field sat low to the ground and provided fans with scores from around the Pacific Coast League using the now-antiquated system of large numbers fitted into boxes denoting scoring inning by inning. It also provided information about the game on the field, charting pitch counts and lineups. This postcard image is one of several that the lovely facility generated.

This ground-level photograph tracks down the right-field line at Gilmore Field, offering a vivid sense of the facility's intimacy. The baselines are extremely close to the seats, and the rows are banked just steeply enough to permit excellent sight lines for everyone in the stands. The press box sat high above the field but was still closer to it than virtually any such seating area in modern stadiums. The field was as accessible to Hollywood as it was to the fans who attended games, so it assumed a second role as a movie set. During its history, Gilmore Field was used in *Meet John Doe* (1941), *It Happened in Flatbush* (1942), *The Stratton Story* (1949), *Kill the Umpire* (1950), and *Pride of St. Louis* (1952). The Hollywood connection was practically limitless. Elizabeth Taylor served as a batgirl for the Stars, and in 1955, Jayne Mansfield was "Miss Hollywood Stars." Chuck Connors, from television's *The Rifleman*, played at Gilmore Field often, as a member of the crosstown rival L.A. Angels.

The Hollywood Stars anticipated the modern-day trend of team mascots by providing cheerleaders at home games. Among those who enjoyed their spirited cheering was one of the Stars' batboys, a lad named Sparky Anderson. He would go on to a short stint in major-league baseball as a player and then a prolific career as a highly successful manager.

Hollywood Stars games were broadcast locally on radio and, in the team's later years, on television as well. In part because of the advent of television, attendance at Gilmore Field began to wane in the 1950s, although crowds still climbed upward of 6,000 or 7,000 fans. Those numbers were typically higher when the L.A. Angels came to Gilmore Field and the rivalry between those two teams remained vital and quite contentious year after year.

This aerial photograph places Gilmore Field in the context of its companions on Gilmore Island. Seen here are Gilmore Stadium directly to the west (at left) and the sites that would host Pan Pacific Auditorium (at right) and Gilmore Drive-In (foreground). For a brief period of time, all of those different venues were open and operating simultaneously. (Photograph by Dick Whittington.)

During a night game, a young woman works the aisles selling cigarettes. It was a day game in which the Stars engaged in a legendary fight with their rival L.A. Angels. The fight lasted a full half-hour. Only when L.A. police chief Bill Parker, watching the game on television, called headquarters from his home and ordered 50 officers to move immediately to the field was the brawl quelled.

The great Joe DiMaggio, the "Yankee Clipper," made an appearance at Gilmore Field. Just as Gilmore Stadium hosted occasional All-Star football games, the Hollywood Stars welcomed major-league stars for exhibitions. Gilmore Field predated the arrival on the West Coast of immigrant teams from the East (the Dodgers, the Giants), so fans got a chance to see the top tier of players.

Babe Ruth appeared at Gilmore Stadium, too. He posed for photographs with two of the Hollywood Stars most popular outfielders, Frank Kelleher (left) and Gus Zernial. Frank Kelleher was at the center of the famous Gilmore Field half-hour brawl, which eventually required LAPD intervention. When a pitch thrown by the rival L.A. Angels' pitcher Joe Hatton hit Kelleher, he charged the mound and every player from both teams poured onto the field. Before it was over, the only players allowed to remain on the field or in the dugouts were those directly involved in the game. Both benches were cleared of all nonessential players, and the dozens of LAPD officers who had stopped the fight took up positions in each dugout until the game finally ended.

Long before baseball's most eccentric general manager, Bill Veeck, put his Chicago White Sox in uniforms featuring shorts, the Hollywood Stars experimented with the concept. Given the greater potential for abrasions from sliding into bases or diving to catch balls, the innovation did not last long. The Stars probably reacted to wearing shorts on the field exactly as the White Sox did years later—they hated it.

This team photograph shows the 1949 Hollywood Stars, the Pacific Coast League champions that year. The team won the league title again in 1952 and 1953; the 1952 team was acknowledged as one of the best minor-league ball clubs of its generation. When the Dodgers came to Los Angeles, the Stars moved to Salt Lake City, but not before 6,000 fans turned out to bid them farewell on September 5, 1957.

83

In 1948, the A. F. Gilmore Company struck a deal with Sero Enterprises and Pacific Theaters to construct a drive-in theater on a section of Gilmore Island facing Third Street. The drive-in was typical in most respects, but it featured one innovation that was unique. It had several rows of benches in front of the parking area, so movie fans who wanted to see a film in the open air could walk in to the drive-in. Despite the drive-in's proximity to a large and growing residential community, neighbors did not take to the walk-in idea and it never quite succeeded with them. With others, however, the drive-in was a hit from its opening, which featured Errol Flynn in *Silver River*. Among those regular patrons was a woman who motored to the movies in her limousine, her chauffeur at the wheel.

The Gilmore Drive-In had another feature that was ideally suited for its time. To accommodate the exploding number of children born to young, postwar parents, the snack shop at the drive-in offered a free baby bottle warming station. This enabled the baby boomer generation to enjoy a double feature with their parents. The Gilmore Drive-In remained open and operating until 1979, making it the most durable of all the attractions and venues that surrounded Farmers Market on Gilmore Island. The theater closed with a double bill, *Naked Riders* and *The Arousers*, and not long after, the handsome entrance, the stylishly modern marquee, the front rows of benches, and the speaker posts were removed.

In 1935, the A. F. Gilmore Company leased a parcel of its original farmland, east of the Gilmore Field site, to a group of entrepreneurs who wanted to build an exhibition hall. The facility was intended to host a National Housing Exhibition, and to meet the deadline for that show Pan Pacific Auditorium was built, from the ground up, in six weeks. The sleek structure, made entirely of wood, had a nautical facade and, for its time, an enormous amount of exhibition space, its interior being 100,000 square feet. Once the housing show closed, the facility continued to be the city's largest exhibition space. It was also used as an entertainment center featuring concerts, dances, sporting events, and circuses. (Photograph by Julius Shulman.)

The Ice Capades were regularly booked into Pan Pacific Auditorium. Other entertainment programs also graced the large facility, including 1957 concerts by Elvis Presley, just months before he was drafted. The shows consisted of his hit songs and lasted about 50 minutes; they drew at least 9,000 people and neighbors reported that they could hear the screaming fans inside the facility from several blocks away.

Hockey was also a regular attraction at Pan Pacific Auditorium, and both amateur clubs and semipro teams played there. For significant periods of time between ice shows and hockey games, the ice rink would remain in place. Residents from the west side of Los Angeles frequented the rink for recreational skating, and lessons were also available.

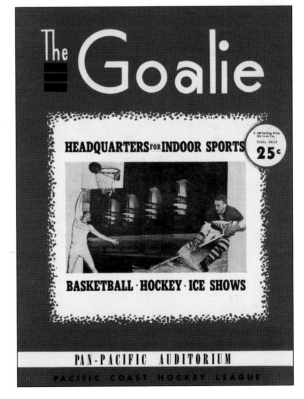

The Goalie

HEADQUARTERS for INDOOR SPORTS   25¢

BASKETBALL · HOCKEY · ICE SHOWS

PAN-PACIFIC AUDITORIUM

PACIFIC COAST HOCKEY LEAGUE

Pan Pacific was more than large enough to accommodate a full circus program and one of the nation's two major circus operations, Clyde Beatty's, appeared in the auditorium on several occasions. These shows neatly mirrored activities at Farmers Market, where Roger Dahlhjelm and Fred Beck frequently brought smaller circuses to the Market's parking lots and hired individual acts—including elephants—for special occasions. Pan Pacific Auditorium remained L.A.'s primary exhibit hall until 1971, when the city built its considerably larger Los Angeles Convention Center downtown. The auditorium stood, unused, for many years until, in 1989, a fire consumed the entire wooden structure in less than two hours.

Five

THE MODERN ERA

Two key events, a decade apart, brought Farmers Market into its modern era.

In 1940, the A. F. Gilmore Company added the Dell to the Market's collection of buildings, directly north of the original Market.

In 1950, E. B. Gilmore demonstrated anew his capacity to anticipate the public's appetite. He razed Gilmore Stadium and after negotiating a deal with CBS to sell the Gilmore land where the stadium had entertained Los Angeles for a more far-reaching diversion, CBS Television City rose where the stadium had stood.

The Dell marked a return to the original concept Roger Dahlhjelm and Fred Beck had presented to E. B. Gilmore. It featured a wide array of small specialty shops adjacent to the original Farmers Market's collection of restaurants and grocery stands.

The CBS deal cemented once and for all the enduring connection between Farmers Market and Hollywood. At the time of that deal, television was predominately a creature of the East Coast, with most production and creative talent centered in New York City. With the construction of the CBS facility, the center of the industry shifted west, bringing with it an economic entertainment machine. In a remarkably short period of time, E. B. Gilmore and CBS moved television production from the East Coast to the West Coast.

A few decades later, the A. F. Gilmore Company again looked to the future, leasing a substantial portion of its remaining land to a developer who created a "life style center," The Grove at Farmers Market, which would change the notion of shopping malls dramatically. At the same time, the Gilmore Company itself undertook significant development, surrounding the original Farmers Market with new structures that, in concert with The Grove at Farmers Market, serve to provide contemporary Los Angeles, and generations to come, with fresh, new incentives to "meet me at Third and Fairfax."

The Dell was a T-shaped building featuring street-level shops that faced Farmers Market and two-story office space fronting Fairfax Avenue. It is seen here from the southwest. CBS Television City is also in the photograph and beyond it one of the last remaining empty sites on the Gilmore property, an old oil drill site. The Dell harkened back to the original idea that spawned Farmers Market. In their original proposal, Roger Dahlhjelm and Fred Beck envisioned shops owned and operated by artisans and, on selected days, farmers in a square vending fresh produce. While the original Farmers Market quickly welcomed merchants other than farmers, the Dell provided a more expansive shopping experience, one much closer to the original concept. (Photograph by Herbert Bruce Cross.)

The Dell, just steps across a sizable parking lot from Farmers Market, offered a mixture of shops and only a couple of food stalls. It did not offer groceries, but it did provide visitors with the chance to browse and purchase such items as stationery, cards, and wrapping paper. This paper shop had a wide collection of supplies for personal and business uses. (Photograph by Rothschild Photos.)

The jewelry store at the Dell offered a complete selection of glittery goods, from costume jewelry to engagement rings and watches; the shop also offered watch repair services. The store was on the easternmost end of the Dell. In later years, jewelry would be available from two shops in the Farmers Market itself, both operated by the Weiss family; the father's store has traditional jewelry and designs, the son's features handmade artistic creations. (Photograph by Rothschild Photos.)

This trinket and souvenir shop in the Dell is typical of the stores that operated there. While the stores had considerably more space than the average Farmers Market stall, they were still small enough to be inviting and intimate. Dell stores tended to be filled with product as shopkeepers took full advantage of their display space to increase sales. (Photograph by Rothschild Photos.)

One of the most popular stores in the Dell was Kip's Toyland. Irwin "Kip" Kipper and his wife, Gerta, opened the shop after his service in World War II; they wanted work that granted them the opportunity to interact with children. The store carried a full range of toys and games, and Kip made a special effort to spot trends and shifts in the appetites of his young customers. (Photograph by Rothschild Photos.)

Irwin "Kip" Kipper, the proprietor of Kip's Toyland, holds a toy. Over the years, Kip developed a strong sense of the value of play as a learning experience—his shop focused on games and toys that required a maximum amount of imagination. He also honed remarkable instincts about the next hot fad among children. He navigated his way from Slinky to Hula Hoop with ease and, on several occasions, anticipated another generation of youngsters who would discover yo-yos. When the Dell closed to make way for newer construction, Kip's Toyland was one of several stores to move into the original Farmers Market. His shop is still there and Kip continues to offer youngsters toys and games that do not have computer screens or electronic handheld control mechanisms.

Barbara Williams, whose father also operated a Farmers Market shop, owned and operated Barbara's Cravats in the Dell. The store carried quality men's clothing and accessories, and it was the source of one of the most remarkable shopping excursions in Farmers Market history. One December in the mid-1950s, entertainer and television star Lee Liberace parked his Cadillac convertible in front of Barbara's store. The flamboyant pianist proceeded to purchase dozens of gifts. He loaded his Cadillac with the purchases, turning the convertible into a veritable Santa's sleigh, and drove away. The shopping spree was so quick that he did not even bother to turn the car off.

Many of the Dell's shops were designed to mirror retail shopping available in smaller community or neighborhood retail districts. This small-town sensibility was evident at Mirandy's, a miniature version of a traditional five-and-dime store. It carried all manner of items from cosmetics and clothing accessories to gifts and souvenirs.

There were some small retail spaces in a building that was between the Dell and Farmers Market from the 1940s until the Market expanded at the turn of the 21st century. The Coral Reef occupied one of those spaces; it is seen here with the Dell in the background. (Photograph by Union Pacific Railroad.)

After the Dell was constructed, a second Farmers Market clock tower was installed atop the structure near its center. The first clock tower, which faced Third Street, was somewhat smaller than this version; the new, larger version dropped the words "An Idea," which graced the older one. Previous icons had served as the visual markers for Farmers Market, a water tower and a windmill both displaying the name from atop Market buildings. They gave way to the clock towers, and over the years the larger clock tower became an internationally recognized symbol of Farmers Market. The contemporary Farmers Market uses a stylized version of the clock tower as its logo on letterhead, envelopes, and promotional materials. When the A. F. Gilmore Company began planning for the addition of new buildings, the Dell's clock tower became a critical part of those plans. It was carefully dismantled and removed, retrofitted to current seismic standards, and placed atop a small retail building that faces the new Market Plaza where it can be seen from the Market's parking lots and surrounding streets. (Photograph by Herbert Bruce Cross.)

In 1955, E. B. Gilmore and the A. F. Gilmore Company created Gilmore Bank. It was intended to be a community bank that would provide financial services and support to the merchants of the Farmers Market and the surrounding community. The bank was designed to convey its mission and its philosophy—it was solid and plain, not showy and daring. The new bank's board of directors is assembled in front of the building on December 2, 1955, to celebrate its grand opening. They are standing in front of the building's Third Street face; on the opposite side of the building is a feature that had become something of a fixture for commercial enterprises of that time—a drive-in window.

Earl Bell Gilmore stands in the rather large vault at the new Gilmore Bank. Although the original concept for the institution called for it to focus on mercantile services, the bank soon expanded its horizons. For a number of decades, Gilmore Bank offered automobile loans at highly attractive rates. These loans were provided in the era before auto manufacturers themselves engaged in financing their own sales and providing terms that were in themselves incentives for purchase. Gilmore Bank's reputation for writing attractive auto loans generated direct referrals from car dealerships all over Los Angeles. The bank also welcomed Farmers Market merchants and they, along with new customers from the immediate neighborhood, grew quickly accustomed to a charming service regime—tellers at Gilmore Bank knew most customers by name and often opened a teller window that served Market merchants exclusively so they could get back to their stalls as quickly as possible.

The original Gilmore Bank was open and spacious. Most of the banks' senior officers maintained desks on the first floor to be available to customers. Designated as a "Commercial and Saving Bank," the institution was, and remains, as cautious as it is friendly. It is consistently listed among the most stable of financial institutions in the nation.

A few of these customers, who started accounts on the day Gilmore Bank opened, still maintain accounts with the institution. When The Grove at Farmers Market was constructed, the original Gilmore Bank building was razed; the "new" Gilmore Bank now anchors one of the property's new buildings, North Market. Some customers protested the destruction of the older building, but the bank itself continues to enjoy loyalty from the community it serves.

This aerial view of Gilmore Island was taken in 1950 when Gilmore Stadium was being razed and CBS Television City was being built. It provides a comprehensive view of the property just before the onset of the Market's modern era. Gilmore Stadium faces Fairfax Avenue on the western edge of the property. Gilmore Field is east of the stadium, and the Dell is to the right of the stadium. Further east is the Pan Pacific Auditorium. The Gilmore Drive-In is on the southern edge of the property. The eccentric collection of buildings facing the corner of Third Street and Fairfax Avenue and extending toward all the other structures that surround it is the original Farmers Market.

Almost as soon as Gilmore Stadium was torn down, CBS began construction on its extensive office building and production studio. The building would eventually serve as a primary television production center in Los Angeles, generating soap operas, situation comedies, and dramas. It also heralded the shift of television's creative center from New York to Los Angeles. Well before he took down Gilmore Stadium, E. B. Gilmore was considering other uses for that site and his negotiations with CBS began at that time. He recognized that Hollywood had vast resources to serve the television age and he understood that a major television production facility immediately next door to Farmers Market would further enhance the Market's long-standing affiliation with the entertainment industry. Given his long, successful career, it is certain that he also recognized that shows produced at the new facility would draw audiences and that those audiences would, inevitably, wander over to the Farmers Market for a meal or some shopping.

CBS Television City was completed within a year and a half and it immediately started drawing audiences to see shows being filmed or taped. No show has had a more dramatic—or amusing—impact on Farmers Market than *The Price Is Right*. Sitting in that show's audience is the only way to get to "come on down" and win prizes. To secure a seat, hopefuls arrive at CBS early in the morning. Once they negotiate the line and secure tickets for one of that day's tapings, they are done with registration by 7:30 or 8:00 a.m. Taping does not commence for several hours. The process generates a Farmers Market phenomenon. Throughout the year, the Farmers Market welcomes parades of bleary folks sporting daffy costumes designed to enhance their chances of being selected to compete for prizes. Some wear matching outfits, couples announce their wedded bliss on T-shirts, and zany hats, odd slogans, and fright wigs are commonplace. Bone tired from their early rise or exhausted from the excitement of the taping, the contestants wander the Market in their unique garb. It is a sight to behold. (Photograph by Julius Shulman.)

By all available evidence, there is something about the machine that churns out fresh peanut butter at Magee's Nuts that politicians find irresistible. It fascinated former president Dwight Eisenhower during a visit to the shop. Years later, Vice Pres. Walter Mondale often contacted the shop to order fresh peanut butter for delivery to the official vice presidential mansion in Washington, D.C.

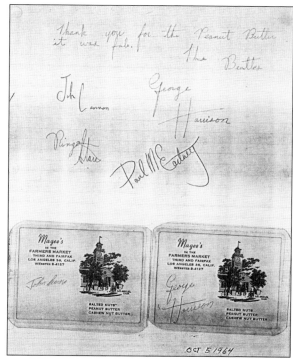

Elected officials are not the only celebrities to be enamored by Magee's Nuts. In the mid-1960s, a rising pop group called The Beatles stopped by for a visit. Upon their return to England, they sent owner Phyllis Magee a handwritten note pronouncing her establishment "fab." If the signatures are a guide, Ringo Starr wrote the note. (Image from Magee's House of Nuts.)

Weis' Feed Rite pet store was a star at Farmers Market for years. Offering pet food and cages, and even a miniature hydrant for the family pup, the shop also had puppies or cats in its display window. The creatures were a major attraction and a source of utter delight for children. While the shop is gone, the family traditions continue—Jack Weis's daughter Ginny and her husband now operate three shops.

Gill's Old Fashioned Ice Cream was among the earliest of the shops to open at Farmers Market. The son of the original owner still serves up desserts and soft drinks from his stand just off the West Patio. Gill's is one of a handful of businesses that have been operating continuously at Farmers Market for decades.

Two phrases echo in the aisles at Farmers Market. The first is, "Gee, I haven't been here in ages . . . it hasn't changed." And the second is, "Does that guy still decorate cakes in the window?" "That guy" is Bill Thee, who operates the shop where his work can still be seen through a picture window. The popular "pink elephant" cake features an inebriated pachyderm clinging to a bottle of champagne.

Another Farmers Market artisan, Michael Graves (right), makes candy by hand and he, too, can be viewed through windows. Typically found up to his elbows in chocolate, Graves started out at the Market in an apprentice-like position and eventually bought Littlejohn's House of English Toffee, where he is one of the last candy makers in the nation working by hand.

Patsy D'Amore was a well-established restaurateur in Los Angeles in the 1940s. His Villa Capri was a Hollywood favorite, welcoming the likes of Frank Sinatra on a regular basis. D'Amore brought two vital innovations to L.A. cuisine—he was the first in town to make and serve a new dish, pizza pie, and he established the region's first pizza parlor at Farmers Market. D'Amore built a brick oven in this shop to bake his pizzas, and that oven is still in place and still turning out great pizza; the shop itself has passed from Patsy to his wife, Rose, and then to their daughter Filomena. The D'Amores are one of several families who operate individual Farmers Market shops—mothers and daughters, fathers and sons, brothers and sisters all work side by side in the Market.

One fixture at Farmers Market, the two-wheel wicker basket, did not survive into the modern era. It was introduced to enable shoppers to shop—like its supermarket cousin, it stored purchases as they were selected. It was unique, however, with only two wheels and a flat base. It was designed to stand upright beside a counter and then roll, being pushed or pulled, to the next stand.

The wooden version of the Farmers Market cart arrived in the 1940s. It is handmade on the property, its official color is "Farmers Market green," and it is popular and peripatetic. To the Market's chagrin, Farmers Market carts wander all over L.A., finding uses as diverse as planters and laundry hampers. In two notorious cases, more than a dozen carts were found in a nearby apartment and one was recently discovered on a sidewalk in Texas.

Roger Dahlhjelm remained the primary force at Farmers Market through the 1940s. He continued to enforce his strict standards and continued to indulge his affection for animals. In addition to keeping a goose named Bill on the property, Dahlhjelm also installed a monkey cage for some time. He toured the property, although not always in a surrey, with his dog Cy.

Hollywood press agents loved using the Farmers Market as a backdrop for publicity shots. In this charming example, Roger Dahlhjelm makes sure that young Natalie Wood enjoys her ice-cream cone. As publicity photographs gave way to television exposure, the Farmers Market adapted, welcoming crews. Dozens of cable and network programs now use the Market to tape segments while local and national news programs frequently visit for "man on the street" interviews.

John Tusquellas operated a successful meat market like this one at the Farmers Market for decades. His son Bob learned a lot from his dad, starting in the family business as the "junior bacon slicer," a job he won because he was too short to see over the counter. The Tusquellas family is one of many whose tenure at the Farmers Market spans generations.

Bob Tusquellas went off to college and returned to Farmers Market as soon as he earned his degree. He purchased a doughnut shop, which quickly became the most popular spot in town for those delicious treats, and eventually assumed management of the family's oyster bar. He also opened a fresh fish market.

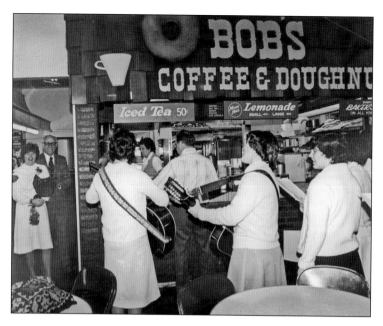

The A. F. Gilmore Company retained John Gostovich as its president when E. B. Gilmore died. Gostovich, the only CEO of the company who was not a member of the Gilmore family, was at least as rigorous in the application of standards for freshness, cleanliness, and presentation as was Roger Dahlhjelm. Here he watches from the far left as a group of nuns serenade customers at Bob's Doughnuts.

Manny Chang made his way from China to Cuba to Los Angeles, where he worked as a caterer/cook at the CBS studios next to the Farmers Market. Eventually Manny and his wife, Angie, opened China Depot. They later expanded their operations to include Bryan's Pit Barbecue, just two stalls down from China Depot; their son Dave now runs the barbecue shop.

Charlie Sue Gilbert worked at Chris's Coffee Shop on the Market's West Patio until its owner retired and Charlie Sue bought the place. She renamed it Charlie's and both her children, Kyle and Katie, work behind the counter with her. A number of Farmers Market enterprises mirror Charlie Sue's experience. Lilian Raymond purchased Coffee Corner after working there (now her children work behind that counter); Clinton Thompson worked as a cook and counterman at the Gumbo Pot and eventually purchased it from its founder, Charles Myers; and Edgar Acosta made crepes for Stephane Strouk before he bought that shop. These shops, side by side with others that have been held in the same family for generations, contribute to a sense of stability, one of the Farmers Market's most endearing qualities. (Photograph by Rothschild Photos.)

No Farmers Market shop exemplifies its stability and integrity more than Magee's Kitchen, the first restaurant on the property. Founders Blanche and Bob Magee were instrumental in the Farmers Market's early development and leaders among the merchants. Blanche passed her restaurant acumen along to her daughter-in-law Phyllis, who has managed the family's restaurant and its nut shop for decades. Roger Dahlhjelm and John Gostovich enforced high standards, but the merchants of the Farmers Market were and remain equally dedicated to quality. Customers at Magee's Nuts have suffered the absence of one of the shop's most popular items, Redskin peanuts, on occasion. When they inquired, they were told that the quality of Redskins available was not up to Magee standards, so Phyllis would not purchase or sell them. Movses Aroyan checks every chicken delivered to his Middle Eastern restaurant, Moishe's, and often rejects as many as he accepts. Bob Tusquellas asks his staff to estimate the number of doughnuts they will sell on any given day, because he refuses to sell any product that is not made fresh on the day it is sold.

Three generations of the DeRosa family have operated Marconda's Meats. The A. F. Gilmore Company remains a family business. Hank Hilty, E. B. Gilmore's grandson, is the current president and CEO, and several members of the next generation work for the company, too. Multigenerational shops include the Gadget Nook, Bryan's Pit Barbecue, Magee's, Charlie Sue's, Coffee Corner, Thee's Continental Bakery, Light My Fire, By Candlelight, Littlejohn's House of English Toffee, Patsy's Pizza, and Sticker Planet.

John Gostovich (center) began serving as the A. F. Gilmore Company CEO in the 1960s, the only person to hold that post who was not a member of the Gilmore family. Here he is seen with Sherif Barsoum (left), who was the Farmers Market's manager for more than 20 years. Their companion is a circus elephant—on several occasions, the Farmers Market used its parking areas to host full circus tents and shows.

There are two main patios at the Farmers Market, the East Patio and the West Patio. Each has its own unique personality and ambiance. The East Patio is home to a legion of "regulars," Farmers Market denizens who spend part of most days there. The East Patio hosts morning coffee regulars, groups occupying "their" mid-morning tables, regular lunch patrons, and mid-afternoon tables filled with regulars who snack and converse as they watch the passing parade. The most famous East Patio regulars are the "Mazursky Table," named for its founder and host, director Paul Mazursky. It is a collection of writers, actors, artists, and producers, and the table has a core of everyday regulars and a stable of frequent visitors. It has been the subject of a BBC documentary and it is a ready source of comment—frequently barbed—for reporters. Recently a producer creating video snapshots of Farmers Market asked the Mazursky Table to discuss their affection for the place. They all agreed. When the producer asked the questions, each at the table responded, all in different foreign languages.

This is the Farmers Market's West Patio in the 1960s. It has its own contingent of regular breakfast diners, including some Charlie Sue Gilbert knows so well that she starts cooking their order when they arrive. Lunch regulars, including several well-known actors, also populate the West Patio. The West Patio is also home to free concerts. The Farmers Market offers two summer music series—Thursday Night Jazz and Friday Night Music—as well as an annual Mardi Gras celebration that features several of the area's finest Cajun bands. That event and the Friday Night Music series were both created by Charles Myers, who founded the Gumbo Pot. He started the Mardi Gras celebration because he thought a restaurant serving New Orleans cuisine was honor bound to let the good times roll. He created the Friday Night Music series to honor the rich cultural heritage of Los Angeles through music. Both the summer series draw large and loyal crowds, and the Mardi Gras celebration is one of the city's most popular parties.

This 1960s vintage shot of a family loading their car with goods from Farmers Market—having used the famous green wooden shopping cart to carry their purchases—is among the most duplicated in the Market's archive. It features the Farmers Market's larger clock tower above the Dell.

Farmers Market celebrated its 60th anniversary in 1994. In addition to a local PBS special honoring the Farmers Market and a live three-hour local morning newscast, the celebration included the presentation of a commendation given to A. F. Gilmore Company president Hank Hilty by Mayor Richard Riordan (right) and Los Angeles City Council president John Ferraro (left). As "Johnny" Ferraro, the councilman played in a college All-Star football game at Gilmore Stadium.

This map was available to Farmers Market visitors in the 1970s. It helped them negotiate the eccentric aisles, nooks, and crannies of the Farmers Market. It is one of many publications provided to visitors over the years, including several newsletters—a *Market Bulletin* that Fred Beck wrote and most recently, the *Bugle*, which began publication in the mid-1990s.

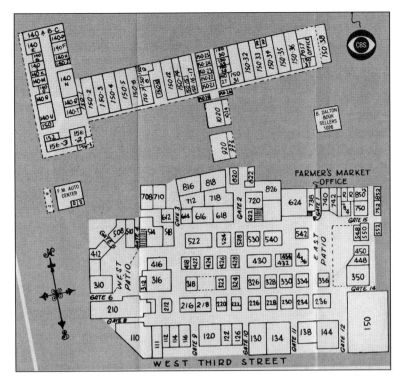

This aerial view of Farmers Market was taken in 1992. Gilmore Stadium had been replaced by the CBS production facility to the north and Gilmore Drive-In was closed, although its footprint is still visible (east of the Farmers Market). The Dell is immediately north of the Market, across the parking lot.

For the 65th anniversary, Los Angeles councilman Tom LaBonge, who succeeded John Ferraro, presented the Farmers Market with a plaque commemorating its contributions to Los Angeles. Like his predecessor, LaBonge is a frequent visitor to the Farmers Market, often lunching on one of the patios with friends and constituents.

In the 1980s, the A. F. Gilmore Company began exploring an expansion on the large areas of undeveloped property surrounding Farmers Market. After much public debate, the company and the City of Los Angeles agreed on a plan to develop The Grove at Farmers Market. The new "life style" center, developed by Rick Caruso, was an instant success, drawing record numbers of visitors and a new and expanded audience to Gilmore Island.

The A. F. Gilmore Company developed new facilities as The Grove at Farmers Market was being built. The Dell was razed to make room for North Market, a modern structure housing retail space on its first floor and office space on its second. The company also created the Market Plaza, a distinctive structure adjacent to the original Farmers Market that has numerous shops and a large, popular patio. (Photograph by Lucy Gonzales.)

This is the contemporary aerial view of Gilmore Island. Farmers Market, on the northeast corner of Third Street and Fairfax Avenue, is framed by the Market Plaza building. To the north, North Market fronts its own parking lot and, to the east, The Grove at Farmers Market—with a multiscreen movie theater, a large department store, numerous shops and stores, and several restaurants—is near the land where Pan Pacific Auditorium once stood. (Photograph by Benny Chan.)

For all the changes that have taken place at Farmers Market, it remains essentially the same. This Christmastime shot of the balcony in front of the Farmers Market offices, taken in 1953, could as easily have been taken yesterday. The balcony has not changed and the shops below are as they have always been. The capacity to adapt and yet retain its essential character is among the Farmers Market's most delightful traits. This characteristic most frequently emerges when visitors return to the Market after long periods of absence. While they almost always enjoy a new discovery—a new shop here or, if their absence has been substantial, the new Market Plaza and North Market—they also relish finding an old favorite shop or restaurant and usually an old friend behind the counter.

The late K. C. Marelich worked for Farmers Market in several capacities. She is pictured here inside the Gilmore Adobe, where she served as the A. F. Gilmore Company's executive assistant. That assignment gave rise to one of the most intriguing aspects of the stability that is at the heart of Farmers Market. Often working in the adobe late into the evening, Marelich became utterly convinced that the spirits of one or both of A. F. Gilmore and E. B. Gilmore roamed around the building. The adobe, built in 1852 and the Gilmore family home until E. B. died in 1964, is now the A. F. Gilmore Company headquarters. The home and its grounds are not open to the public, although the extensive lawns are used for occasional charitable events and company festivities. It may also be the home of the real reason that Farmers Market remains true to its heritage and steadfastly constant—the late Gilmore gentlemen are making sure of that by keeping an eye on the place.

Arthur Fremont Gilmore (left) and Earl Bell Gilmore appear in these portraits. Both spent their lives nurturing, enhancing, and respecting the large expanse of property that A. F. Gilmore "won" by drawing a straw. A. F. Gilmore turned the property into a successful dairy farm, discovered its rich oil reserves, and turned it into an oil field, which contributed to the growth of Los Angeles and the West. E. B. Gilmore turned the oil enterprise into a major economic force, built the family business into a far-reaching and forward-thinking enterprise, and helped Roger Dahlhjelm and Fred Beck bring their idea for a farmers' market to life.

In the 1940s, Farmers Market promoted itself with a bold pronouncement that was absolutely true: it was world famous. For many years, it was the number-one tourist attraction in Southern California. Today it draws millions of visitors annually from across the United States and from around the world. It is a common experience to wander the aisles and hear visitors speaking French, German, Japanese, Spanish, and to hear English spoken with a rich British or Australian accent. Throughout the year, large coach busses arrive and open their doors to visitors from everywhere. During the holiday season, Rose Bowl fans flock to Farmers Market in such numbers that it is necessary to secure additional bus parking to accommodate them. Television programs from Europe, Asia, and South America routinely come to the Farmers Market to tape segments. The Farmers Market may become more world famous in the years to come, but it is long past "becoming" so.

Standing on the Market Plaza and looking east toward The Grove at Farmers Market, the property's history is not readily evident. A trolley now shuttles visitors between the two, following a path that was almost certainly trod by a herd of dairy cows a century ago. The Gilmore Drive-In is long gone, but the cinema complex that now draws fans is almost exactly on the site where that theater once stood. Gilmore Field would have been just a bit north of The Grove at Farmers Market's tall parking structure, close enough for those parking on the top level to look out on a baseball game. The history may not be evident, yet it infuses the entire experience. Farmers Market is the same wonderfully eclectic and eccentric grocery store, dining room, and meeting space it has always been. The Grove at Farmers Market is the latest, and arguably the most magnetic, of a long line of attractions that have drawn people to and enhanced their experience at Farmers Market.

In the 1990s, as part of a renovation of the Market's West Patio, the A. F. Gilmore Company opened a beer and wine bar. To honor the company's heritage and to pay tribute to the man who supported an idea from Roger Dahlhjelm and Fred Beck, the bar was named E. B.'s Beer and Wine. It is one of two tributes to Earl Bell Gilmore; the other being the replica of a 1936 Gilmore gas station, Earl's Service, near the Market Plaza. With the arrival of E. B.'s Beer and Wine, the West Patio has become a center for Farmers Market entertainment. On Thursday and Friday nights—and on special occasions such as Mardi Gras and St. Patrick's Day—bands provide free concerts to Farmers Market patrons of all ages who enjoy music with their dinners.

In January 2009, as Farmers Market launched a yearlong celebration of its 75th anniversary, a new manager arrived. Stan Savage, a direct descendant of A. F. and E. B. Gilmore, initiated his new duties by doing precisely what Roger Dahlhjelm and Fred Beck had done three-quarters of a century ago: he started searching for farmers who would join the merchants in Farmers Market to sell just-picked fruits and vegetables to shoppers. The farmers who responded to the call are exactly like those who populated Farmers Market in July 1934. They grow their produce, bring it to the corner of Third Street and Fairfax Avenue in trucks, and happily serve their customers the best they can offer, just as Farmers Market merchants have done all along. Thus, 75 years after it opened, Farmers Market is still true to its roots, still devoted to its traditions, and still a wonderful place to shop and visit. It has changed, yet it has remained the same friendly, cherished destination it was from its first days.

While there were not yet patios in 1934 when Farmers Market was created, it still offered a welcome respite from the Great Depression, a place where folks could leave the hard times behind and enjoy a visit to a warm and simple place that was friendly and comfortable. In 2009, as the economy once again turned sour and the Farmers Market celebrates its 75th anniversary, the same amiable, comfortable atmosphere and ambiance draws locals and visitors still, welcoming people who seek relief from the stress of the day over a cup of coffee, a conversation with friends, and a warm, sunny place to relax. Over the years, Farmers Market has sustained and comforted millions of visitors. It is L.A.'s favorite place and, if history is an accurate barometer, it will continue to be so for a long, long time.

www.arcadiapublishing.com

MAP SEARCH

Discover books about the town where you grew up, the cities where your friends and families live, the town where your parents met, or even that retirement spot you've been dreaming about. Our Web site provides history lovers with exclusive deals, advanced notification about new titles, e-mail alerts of author events, and much more.

MADE IN THE USA

Arcadia Publishing, the leading local history publisher in the United States, is committed to making history accessible and meaningful through publishing books that celebrate and preserve the heritage of America's people and places. Consistent with our mission to preserve history on a local level, this book was printed in South Carolina on American-made paper and manufactured entirely in the United States.

This book carries the accredited Forest Stewardship Council (FSC) label and is printed on 100 percent FSC-certified paper. Products carrying the FSC label are independently certified to assure consumers that they come from forests that are managed to meet the social, economic, and ecological needs of present and future generations.

FSC
Mixed Sources
Product group from well-managed forests and other controlled sources

Cert no. SW-COC-001530
www.fsc.org
© 1996 Forest Stewardship Council

Find Your Place in History.